best ever

pasta

p

This is a Parragon Publishing Book
First published in 2003

Parragon Publishing
Queen Street House
4 Queen Street
Bath BA1 1HE
United Kingdom

Created and produced by
The Bridgewater Book Company Ltd,
Lewes, East Sussex

Photographer Ian Parsons
Home economists Sara Hesketh and Richard Green

ISBN: 1–40542–046–4

Printed in China

NOTE

This book uses imperial, metric, or US cup measurements. Follow the same
units of measurement throughout; do not mix imperial and metric. All spoon
measurements are level: teaspoons are assumed to be 5 ml and tablespoons are
assumed to be 15 ml. Unless otherwise stated, milk is assumed to be whole,
eggs and individual vegetables such as potatoes are medium, and pepper is
freshly ground black pepper.

The times given for each recipe are an approximate guide only.
The preparation times may differ according to the techniques used by different
people and the cooking times may vary as a result of the type of oven used.
Ovens should be preheated to the specified temperature. If using a fan-assisted
oven, check the manufacturer's instructions for adjusting the time and temperature.
The preparation times include chilling and marinating times, where appropriate.

The nutritional information provided for each recipe is per serving or per
portion. Optional ingredients, variations, or serving suggestions have not been
included in the calculations.

Recipes using raw or very lightly cooked eggs should be avoided
by infants, the elderly, pregnant women, convalescents, and anyone
suffering from an illness.

contents

introduction

Whatever your tastes, there is a type of pasta to suit you and your family. If you are trying to lose weight or eat more healthily, pasta is ideal and can be invaluable as a lowfat staple of your diet. It is popular with children and you can let them eat it as often as they like since it is low in sugar, salt, and fat. Plain pasta dishes, such as macaroni with butter or cheese, are excellent for people who are unwell, and more complicated dishes including meat, poultry, or seafood with herbs and spices can be served when you are feeding a hungry family or you want to impress.

Popular folklore has it that Marco Polo introduced pasta to Italy in the 13th century when he brought it back from China, but there is evidence that both countries were very familiar with pasta long before his time. Some Italian historians have claimed that the Etruscans made pasta, predating the Chinese who are thought to have started making noodles around the first century AD.

choosing ingredients

Almost any ingredient can be incorporated into a pasta dish or added to a sauce. Some of the best-known dishes, such as Classic Tagliatelle Bolognese (see page 62), Lasagna al Forno (see page 70), and Spaghetti alla Puttanesca (see page 34), have beef or seafood as the main ingredient—apart from the pasta—and you can use many different types of seafood or cuts of meat. Depending on your pantry, you can create your own variations on well-known, tried-and-tested recipes. Pasta is very versatile and there are many shapes and colors readily available to make an attractive lunch or dinner. You can add more or less any vegetable to a pasta dish, creating a nutritious and filling meal. This also makes sense economically, as you can use whatever vegetables are in season, which will be less expensive. Sauces can be based round popular, familiar vegetables, such as zucchini, tomatoes, or onions, or you can experiment with more unusual combinations, such as pumpkin and sun-dried tomatoes. Pasta is also a very healthy choice for vegetarians, who can add variety to their diet with different types of pasta combined with sauces or simply baked with cheese.

versatility and variety

Many pasta dishes are made with fresh ground beef, but there are plenty of other options. Fish in a creamy sauce is a wonderful alfresco summer lunch, served with fresh salad and a glass of white wine, and can be surprisingly light, depending on the type of pasta used. Scallops and crabmeat, for example, are wonderfully complemented by pasta. Eggs, raw or hard-cooked and chopped, can be added to many sauces as an alternative or in addition to meat. While there are more exotic ingredients to experiment with, cheese and cream sauces are still among the tastiest ways of serving pasta. Whatever you have in the pantry, refrigerator, or freezer—chicken, cheese, mushrooms, or bacon—you will find a suitable pasta dish to cook for a hungry family or an intimate lunch.

Pasta is wonderfully adaptable and you can see just how flexible it is from the range of recipes in this book. Not only are there many different ways of incorporating it into a dish, but there are different colors and flavors, as well as a huge variety of sauces. You can use the same pasta shapes and very similar ingredients and still end up with totally different dishes. Pasta can be boiled, baked, added to soups, made into salads, served as a main dish, or used in a side dish.

cooking with pasta

There is a huge range of recipes featured in this book, from exotic dishes perfect for entertaining to simple, quick, and easy dishes for a family supper. Some of the ingredients used are fresh and will have to be bought especially for the dish, others can be found in most pantries and refrigerators. Pasta dishes can be as rich and filling as a winter stew or as light and summery as a salad. Pasta works well in soups and can add a lovely color if you use a variety flavored with beet or spinach. Italian Chicken Soup (see page 26) and Fish Soup with Anellini (see page 28) are both delicious and make an ideal summer lunch. There are many light meals featured that make great lunches or evening snacks or can be served as a preliminary dish before the main course in the Italian style. Tagliatelle with Walnuts (see page 47) has a creamy walnut flavor. There are traditional, well-known dishes, such as Spaghetti &

Meatballs (see page 65) and the newly fashionable Penne with Chicken & Arugula (see page 114). Lasagna, a perennially popular dish, can be made with meat as in the Mixed Meat Lasagna (see page 72), without meat as in Vegetable Lasagna (see page 223), with seafood as in the Lasagna alla Marinara (see page 136), or you could even try the Chicken Lasagna (see page 96). Dishes such as Linguine with Clams in Tomato Sauce (see page 161) or Pappardelle with Asparagus (see page 214) are ideal for entertaining.

It is hardly surprising that most of the recipes featured here are Italian, but there are a few different dishes from Greece and France. Italian cooking varies from region to region, so many local specialties are included. There are classics from Milan, such as Minestrone Milanese (see page 18) and Tuscan Chicken Tagliarini (see page 113) from Tuscany, the olive oil capital of the world. Campania, with its wealth of vegetables and fish, is represented by Spaghetti con Vongole (see page 162), while Bologna's signature dish, Classic Tagliatelle Bolognese (see page 62), could hardly be omitted. There are also Roman dishes, such as Tagliarini all'Alfredo (see page 54), and Sicilian ones—try Sicilian Linguine (see page 77), a delicious mixture of beef, eggplant, tomatoes, and olives.

There are four chapters in this book and you can mix and match the recipes. *Soups & Light Meals* suggests dishes for a lunch, appetizer, or light evening meal. You can use many of these recipes as side dishes, adapting them according to your taste and the number of guests you are expecting. The second chapter, *Meat & Poultry*, features many dishes that would be delicious on a cold wintry night, but they can just as easily be served in the middle of summer. *Fish & Shellfish* is a great chapter for entertaining, as seafood dishes combined with colored pasta look fabulous. Many of the recipes are very simple to make, but look as if you have spent hours cooking over a hot stove. *Vegetables & Salads* can be a lifesaver for those with vegetarian friends.

If you live in a meat-eating household and have vegetarian visitors, these dishes provide variety and color for very little extra effort and will be enjoyed by everyone. Pasta salads are ideal for summer, providing a change from lettuce, and they make great barbecue side dishes.

health and convenience

All the recipes in this book were written with health considerations in mind and most can be easily adapted to suit different requirements as well as different palates, without losing the essence of the dish.

Pasta is very economical and it is easy to make an inexpensive and tasty dish with few ingredients, especially if you grow your own vegetables or live near a well-stocked market. If you are boiling rather than baking pasta, then it is also fast to cook, some types taking as little as 4–5 minutes. Fresh pasta cooks very fast and dried pasta takes only a little longer. You can also precook pasta to use in a salad, saving more time and making a tasty summer dish.

Often the choice for many athletes and health-conscious people, pasta is healthy and nutritious. Whole-wheat pasta is available, providing an alternative for the fiber-conscious. Although it is often thought to be fattening, this is untrue. It is an excellent complex carbohydrate, which releases energy steadily, and is recommended by nutritionists. On the other hand, many pasta sauces are cooked with oil and include large amounts of cheese or cream and it is these that pile on the calories. Many of the dishes featured here are suitable for a lowfat diet, while those that aren't can be adapted to suit your requirements. Substitute lowfat creams and yogurt and cook in good-quality, heavy-bottom or non-stick pans with little or no added fat to make these meals low in fat. Most of the recipes specify olive oil, which is high in monounsaturated fats and is thought to lower blood cholesterol levels, as well as having a unique flavor.

types of pasta

There are many different shapes, colors, and flavors of pasta available and you may have a choice of fresh (*pasta fresca*) or dried (*pasta secca*). Pasta can be made from many different ingredients, including soft wheat, durum wheat, buckwheat, mung beans, soybeans, and rice. These last three ingredients are used mainly in Asian countries. In Italy, there is variation from one region to another. Hard durum wheat is the preferred grain in southern Italy and works well for dried pasta, which has a longer cooking time than fresh. In northern Italy, fettuccine, linguine, and tagliatelle are traditionally made with softer wheat flour and mixed with egg, producing pasta with a much faster cooking time.

There are about 200 different pasta shapes and about 600 different names for them. If you are lucky enough to visit Italy, you will find that a shape may have one name in one region and a different name in another. Some pasta shapes are best served with certain sauces or types of sauces, but there is nothing stopping you from substituting your own homemade pasta shapes or the ones that you prefer. Thick, creamy sauces are often best served with long ribbons of pasta, as they will just coat the strands. Seafood sauces are served with long, thin pastas, such as spaghetti or vermicelli. Vegetable sauces should be served with shells or similar shapes that will hold some sauce with every mouthful. Every recipe suggests a type of pasta, but this is not a hard-and-fast rule.

There are also different colors of pasta available as well as different shapes. You will find that the colored varieties are most often long ribbons, but you can buy colored fusilli (spirals) and conchiglie (shells) as well. The reddish orange of pasta flavored with tomato is familiar to most people and is a firm favorite with children. The flavor is not strong and is usually served with a tomato-based sauce. Spinach is also frequently used as a flavoring and provides a vibrant green color to liven up any dish. This is often paired with plain or tomato pasta for an interesting and attractive contrasting effect. Pasta tricolore is a mixture of plain, tomato, and spinach. Beet is a less familiar flavoring than spinach or tomato, but is very attractive with a pleasant, mild flavor. Cuttlefish or squid ink provides a dramatic black for some pasta dishes, yet will not spoil the flavor of delicate sauces. Served in many expensive restaurants, black pasta can be hard to find in the supermarket and you may need to seek out an Italian delicatessen or make it yourself. Golden brown pasta can be flavored with exotic mushrooms for a real treat.

Colored pasta looks very impressive when entertaining and is usually no more expensive than plain. A lovely way to present a pasta dish is to cook two different colors of the same type separately and place them side by side on the plate before topping with your chosen sauce. Although some dishes are made with a particular pasta, such as Classic Tagliatelle Bolognese (see page 62), you can use any color and flavor you like. Most of the recipes do not specify a particular color, but there are a few exceptions, such as Paglia e Fieno with Garlic Crumbs (see page 36), literally "straw and hay."

Some of the long, thin, ribbon-style pasta available include tagliatelle, tagliarini, fettuccine, and the broader pappardelle. The best-known thin pasta is spaghetti, but there are many other types from the very fine capelli d'angelo (angel hair), spaghettini, and vermicelli to the thicker bucatini. These types of pasta can often be bought fresh or dried, rolled into small "nests."

Many small shapes are available dried and you may also find some fresh. Conchiglie (shells), penne (quills), farfalle (bows), macaroni, and fusilli (spirals) are probably the best known, but there are also many others from gemelli (twins) to strozzapretti (priest stranglers). Short, fat tubes, such as pipe and rigatoni, are also relatively easy to find and make an attractive change. Many of

these are available made from whole-wheat flour and are ideal for cold pasta salads and for children, who also love alphabet and animal shapes.

Filled pasta is popular and easy, especially if bought fresh and served with a simple sauce. Ravioli (squares) and agnolotti (crescents) are well known and the easiest filled pasta to make at home. The filled shapes of plain or colored pasta can be cooked in boiling water for a few minutes and served with a tomato and herb sauce for an inexpensive and filling meal. Tortellini are small knots of pasta and are good served with zucchini and bell pepper or tomato sauces. Cappelletti (little hats) and caramellone (toffees) are fun shapes, good with rich tomato or creamy sauces. The best place to buy ready-made filled pasta is an Italian delicatessen, but nothing beats homemade. Try Spinach & Ricotta Ravioli (see page 228) or Chicken & Bacon Tortellini (see page 102).

Lots of very small pasta shapes are widely available for adding to homemade soups, providing both texture and substance. These include stellete (stars), anelli (rings), seme di peperone (pepper seeds), and risi (rice grains).

There are new "designer" pasta shapes being made all the time—canned spaghetti, however nasty, is the perfect example of this. Alphabet spaghetti is still very popular among children and a range of shapes and characters has been added to this category. Dried pasta is becoming increasingly available in new shapes and many of these are ideal for fussy children and for adults with a sense of humor.

homemade pasta

Fresh pasta is available in the chiller cabinets of most supermarkets and is easy, if slightly time-consuming, to make at home. Many people prefer fresh pasta and it is worth buying if it is well-made filled pasta, which you will find at an Italian delicatessen. Dried pasta is often thought of as being more convenient, but packaged fresh pasta is, in fact, faster and easier to prepare. Some varieties of fresh pasta can take as little as 3–4 minutes to cook, while dried pasta will usually take at least double this. Some types of pasta, mainly tubular shapes, are only sold dried. Others, including lasagna, linguine, tagliatelle, and fettuccine, are sold in both fresh and dried forms, offering the cook more choice.

Commercially produced pasta is made using a machine and the dough is shaped by metal rollers, which are made from Teflon or stainless steel, giving the pasta a smooth texture and appearance. Homemade machines usually clamp to the counter and the dough can be made by hand or in a food processor.

If you choose to make fresh pasta at home, you will reap the benefits of your hard work. You should make sure that you have the appropriate equipment handy before you start to make your dough, including the obvious things, such as clean mixing bowls, a cutting board, a sharp knife, measuring spoons, and a rolling pin. There are several other pieces of equipment designed to make pasta-making easier, and some of these, such as a pasta or pastry wheel, are essential if you are making pasta with a decorated edge. Although pasta can be rolled by hand, investing in a pasta machine will save time and make the job much easier. Various attachments for different shapes are available with some models. If you are going to make ravioli, then a ravioli cutter or set of pastry cutters will be very useful, as will a ravioli tray.

cooking pasta

One of the wonderful things about pasta is that, once you have got to grips with a couple of rules, anybody can cook it. It is almost impossible to burn, and if the worst comes to the worst and something does go wrong, you can throw it away and start again, as it is inexpensive and fast

to cook. Unfilled fresh pasta is cooked the same way as plain dried pasta, but make sure that the cooking time is reduced according to the package instructions.

For all types, make sure that the water is boiling before you add the pasta. You need a large pan of water and it should be lightly salted. The general guidelines for the amount of water to use are as follows: 4 quarts of water and 3 tablespoons of salt for every 10½ oz–1 lb/300–450 g of dried or fresh pasta. This will ensure that the pasta does not stick and will not boil dry. Do not cover the pan or the water will boil over. Some cooks like to add 1 tablespoon of oil in the belief that this will prevent the pasta sticking, but it is not necessary. For a main course dish, allow about 5½ oz/150 g of fresh pasta or 3½ oz/100 g of dried pasta per person, but quantities will vary depending on the sauce.

Add all the pasta to the boiling water and stir once to prevent sticking. Return to a boil and continue to boil, not simmer, until the pasta is cooked. When ready, the pasta should be *al dente*, which means "to the tooth," or firm to the bite. It should retain its shape, but should not feel hard in the center. The easiest way to test it is to bite a small piece.

Drain the pasta immediately using a large colander. Rinse with boiling water to prevent sticking, if you like, or with cold water if the dish requires cold pasta. Serve immediately, tossed in butter or olive oil or with a sauce. If the pasta has to stand while you finish the sauce, toss it in a little olive oil first. Given the choice, make the sauce wait for the pasta.

Finally, remember that cooking times apply only after the water has returned to a boil, once the pasta has been added:

- Fresh, unfilled pasta will take only 2–3 minutes to cook, although some very fine ribbons may be ready as soon as the water has boiled again.
- Dried, unfilled pasta will take 8–12 minutes to cook. Refer to the package instructions for unusual shapes or sizes and check frequently.
- Fresh, filled pasta will take 8–10 minutes to cook, while dried, filled pasta will cook in 15–20 minutes.

essential ingredients

Parmesan cheese is often added to many different pasta dishes. Choose good-quality cheese. Buy cheese fresh and in small quantities and grate it yourself just before using. Pecorino cheese is also excellent for grating, as it is hard and only a little is needed for a wonderful flavor.

Other useful cheeses include ricotta, a soft, creamy whey cheese often partnered with spinach; Gorgonzola, a piquant blue cheese; dolcelatte, a creamy, milder blue cheese; and feta, which is a Greek ewe's milk cheese.

There is a huge variety of mushrooms available and experimenting with different flavors can be enjoyable. Some are available fresh and dried and you may be lucky enough to live where they grow wild. If you pick your own mushrooms, make sure that you can identify them accurately before cooking and eating. Cultivated white mushrooms are the type most widely available and one of the least expensive. White mushrooms are best used whole. Chanterelle mushrooms have a delicate flavor and golden appearance. They are usually available fresh or dried and are concave. Brush off dirt rather than washing these mushrooms, as they are porous. Cremini mushrooms are very similar and have a firm texture and strong flavor. They are ideal for adding flavor to sauces. Morel mushrooms are becoming widely used and are available fresh or dried. Leave morels soaking in salted water for 2 minutes to remove any insects, then rinse under cold running water. Pat dry with paper towels and use whole or sliced. Porcini mushrooms, also known as cèpes, are available fresh and dried. The dried varieties are useful when a concentrated flavor is needed, as in many pasta sauces. Oyster mushrooms are sold fresh and have an attractive fluted shape. They can be used in most dishes but release a lot of moisture during cooking. Portobello mushrooms are large and tasty and are best served relatively plain.

Olive oil is a very important ingredient in Italian cooking, and whole or chopped olives are also used in abundance. Olive trees have been grown in the Mediterranean for over 6,000 years, making them the oldest cultivated tree in existence. Olives are available in many different colors, green and black being the most familiar. You may also find pink or violet olives or those that are a combination of colors.

Delicious sauces can be made using olives and olive oil, and black olives will add a beautiful deep color to pasta sauces. Italian olives have exotic-sounding names, such as Rosciolo, Biancolilla, and Frantoio, but most supermarket-bought olives are suitable for making sauce. Olives can be stored in the refrigerator for convenience, but should be served at room temperature. Add to dishes toward the end of cooking so that the flavor permeates throughout the sauce, but the olives retain their texture.

Olive oil is a healthy choice and has about 77 percent monounsaturated fat, as opposed to some other cooking oils and butter, which can be high in saturated fats. Olive oil can be added to the pan before any other ingredient or can be drizzled over cooked pasta as a finishing touch. For general cooking purposes, use virgin olive oil, as this is less expensive than the finer extra virgin olive oil. Set aside your finest and most expensive extra virgin oil for dressings and finishing touches where the flavor can be properly appreciated. Store olive oil away from light in a cool cupboard.

fresh flavors

There are many different kinds of herbs and most are easy to grow in your garden or in a window box. Fresh herbs should always be used in preference to dried, where possible, as they have a much finer flavor and color, although you will need a larger quantity. Basil is a commonly used herb in Italy and goes particularly well with tomatoes, making it the ideal herb to use for pasta sauces. A simple tomato and basil sauce will be delicious served with ravioli or as a quick and easy spaghetti sauce. It is also an essential ingredient in pesto, a Genoese sauce. Basil does not dry well, so if the fresh herb is not available, use a spoonful of pesto instead. Tarragon pairs well with chicken; use a creamy tarragon sauce with either chicken or fish. Dill and chervil are usually used with salmon, but will work well with all seafood and in pasta salads. Parsley will go well with almost anything, and particularly with chicken and fish, although it can be added as a garnish to any dish before serving. Flatleaf parsley, also known as Italian parsley, is traditional. Rosemary has a very strong flavor and should be used sparingly, although it goes well with baked pasta dishes and adds a wonderful aroma. Sage is a natural partner for chicken and can be used sparingly in creamy

pasta sauces. Chives provide a strong flavor and attractive color that goes well with seafood dishes with creamy sauces and strongly flavored tomato and meat sauces. Fresh chives are far superior to dried. Oregano and marjoram are closely related herbs and traditionally flavor many meat sauces for pasta. Garlic is a must-have and is used in most dishes. Long cooking, such as roasting, gives it a mellow flavor, but do not burn it when you are sautéing because it will taste bitter.

Fresh vegetables in season, whether fennel, eggplant, zucchini, bell peppers, or spinach, are the hallmark of Italian cooking. Beans and tomatoes feature widely in pasta dishes and they do not have to be fresh. Canned beans are easier and more convenient than dried, and canned tomatoes are an invaluable pantry basic. Resist the urge to buy the cheapest brand, as it is likely to be watery. Canned chopped tomatoes are usually more substantial than whole ones. Other useful tomato products include tomato paste, a strong concentrate, and strained tomatoes. When buying fresh tomatoes, look for sun-ripened specimens, which will have a sweeter, fuller flavor than those grown under glass. Plum tomatoes are traditionally used in Italy and are less watery than standard tomatoes. Sun-dried tomatoes are available in packages or bottled in oil. Reconstitute packaged tomatoes with hot water and drain bottled ones. The oil from the jar may be used for extra flavoring. Sun-dried tomato paste adds an intense flavor to sauces.

Pine nuts may be used in sauces and as a garnish. They are an essential ingredient in pesto sauce. Walnuts are also widely used. *Panna da cucina* or "cooking cream" is widely used in Italy and is more or less the equivalent of heavy cream. Pancetta is an Italian bacon that adds depth of flavor to many pasta sauces. It may be smoked or unsmoked and is usually quite fatty. Lean bacon is an adequate substitute, if you cannot find pancetta.

Discover more about Italian ingredients to enhance your pasta dishes by browsing around a good Italian delicatessen. You may even be offered samples to taste!

basic recipes

vegetable stock

makes: 8 cups
preparation time: 20 minutes
cooking time: 35 minutes

2 tbsp corn oil
4 oz/115 g onions, finely chopped
4 oz/115 g leeks, finely chopped
4 oz/115 g carrots, finely chopped
4 celery stalks, finely chopped
3 oz/85 g fennel, finely chopped
3 oz/85 g tomatoes, finely chopped
generous 2¼ quarts water
1 bouquet garni

1 Heat the oil in a pan. Add the onions and leeks and cook over low heat, stirring occasionally, for 5 minutes, or until softened. Add the remaining vegetables, cover, and cook for 10 minutes. Add the water and bouquet garni, bring to a boil, and let simmer for 20 minutes.

2 Strain, let cool, and store in the refrigerator. Use immediately or freeze in portions for up to 3 months.

fish stock

makes: 6 cups
preparation time: 10 minutes
cooking time: 30 minutes

1 lb 7 oz/650 g white fish heads, bones
and trimmings, rinsed
1 onion, sliced
2 celery stalks, chopped
1 carrot, sliced
1 bay leaf
4 fresh parsley sprigs
4 black peppercorns
½ lemon, sliced
6 cups water
½ cup dry white wine

1 Place the fish pieces in a pan. Add the remaining ingredients. Bring to a boil, skimming off the foam that rises to the surface. Reduce the heat, partially cover, and let simmer for 25 minutes.

2 Strain, without pressing down on the contents of the strainer. Cool and store in the refrigerator. Use at once or freeze in portions for up to 3 months.

chicken stock

makes: generous 2½ quarts
preparation time: 15 minutes,
plus 30 minutes chilling
cooking time: 3½ hours

3 lb/1.3 kg chicken wings and necks
2 onions, cut into wedges
4 quarts water
2 carrots, coarsely chopped
2 celery stalks, coarsely chopped
10 fresh parsley sprigs
4 fresh thyme sprigs
2 bay leaves
10 black peppercorns

1 Place the chicken wings and necks and the onions in a pan and cook over low heat, stirring frequently, until browned all over. Add the water and stir to scrape off any sediment on the bottom of the pan. Bring to a boil, skimming off the scum that rises to the surface. Add the remaining ingredients, partially cover, and let simmer for 3 hours.

2 Strain, let cool, and place in the refrigerator. When cold, discard the layer of fat on the surface. Use immediately or freeze in portions for up to 6 months.

beef stock

makes: 7 cups
preparation time: 15 minutes,
plus 30 minutes chilling
cooking time: 4½ hours

2 lb 4 oz/1 kg beef marrow bones,
sawn into 3-inch/7.5-cm pieces
1 lb 7 oz/650 g stewing beef in 1 piece
3 quarts water
4 cloves
2 onions, halved
2 celery sticks, coarsely chopped
8 peppercorns
1 bouquet garni

1 Place the bones in the bottom of a large pan and place the stewing beef on top. Add the water and bring to a boil over low heat, skimming off the scum that rises to the surface. Press a clove into each onion half and add to the pan with the celery, peppercorns, and bouquet garni. Partially cover and let simmer gently for 3 hours. Remove the meat and let simmer for an additional 1 hour.

2 Strain, let cool, and place in the refrigerator. When cold, discard the layer of fat on the surface. Use immediately or freeze in portions for up to 6 months.

béchamel sauce

makes: 1¼ cups
preparation time: 20 minutes
cooking time: 20 minutes

1¼ cups milk
1 bay leaf
6 black peppercorns
slice of onion
mace blade
2 tbsp butter
scant ¼ cup all-purpose flour
salt and pepper

1 Pour the milk into a pan and add the bay leaf, peppercorns, onion, and mace. Heat gently to just below boiling point, then remove from the heat, cover, and let infuse for 10 minutes. Strain the milk into a pitcher.

2 Melt the butter in a separate pan. Sprinkle in the flour and cook over low heat, stirring constantly, for 1 minute. Remove from the heat and gradually stir in the milk. Return to the heat and bring to a boil, stirring. Cook, stirring, until thickened and smooth. Season to taste with salt and pepper.

basic pasta dough

serves: 3–4
preparation time: 10 minutes,
plus 30 minutes resting

This is the most basic recipe for making
pasta dough by hand. You can add
colorings and flavorings according to
the dish (see below).

**generous 1¼ cups all-purpose flour
or strong white bread flour,
plus extra for dusting
pinch of salt
2 eggs, lightly beaten
1 tbsp olive oil**

1 Sift the flour and salt onto a clean
counter and make a well in the
center. Pour the eggs and oil into the well,
then using your fingers, gradually combine
the eggs and oil and incorporate the flour.

2 Turn out the dough onto a lightly
floured counter and knead until
smooth. Wrap the dough in plastic wrap
and let rest for at least 30 minutes before
rolling out or feeding through a pasta
machine, as this makes it more elastic. Use
as required.

basic pasta dough in a food processor

serves: 3–4
preparation time: 10 minutes,
plus 30 minutes resting

Pasta made using a food processor is
just as good as handmade, but takes
some of the ache out of the muscles.

**generous 1¼ cups all-purpose flour
or strong white bread flour,
plus extra for dusting
pinch of salt
2 eggs, lightly beaten
1 tbsp olive oil**

1 Sift the flour into the bowl of the
food processor and add the salt.

2 Pour in the eggs and olive oil and
any flavoring and process until the
dough starts to come together.

3 Turn out the dough onto a lightly
floured counter and knead until
smooth. Wrap the dough in plastic wrap
and let rest for at least 30 minutes before
rolling out or feeding through a pasta
machine, as this makes it more elastic. Use
as required.

flavored pasta

tomato pasta: Add 2 tablespoons
tomato paste to the flour when making the
dough and use 1½ eggs instead of 2.

beet pasta: Add 2 tablespoons
grated cooked beet to the flour and use
about 1½ eggs.

saffron pasta: Soak an envelope of
powdered saffron in 2 tablespoons hot
water for 15 minutes. Use 1½ eggs and
whisk the saffron water into them.

herb pasta: Add 3 tablespoons chopped
fresh herbs to the flour.

spinach pasta: Squeeze out
as much liquid as possible from generous
¾ cup thawed frozen spinach or
5 cups fresh spinach blanched in boiling
water for 1 minute. Chop finely
and mix thoroughly with the flour.

whole-wheat pasta: Use 1 cup
whole-wheat flour sifted with scant ¼ cup
all-purpose flour and use 2 eggs.

using a pasta machine: Cutting pasta
by hand can be fun and rewarding if you
have the time, but pasta machines are easy
to use and save a lot of effort. There are
several different models on the market to
suit all budgets and most are simple and
efficient. Pasta machines make ideal
wedding gifts for those interested in
cooking and will last for years if used
and cared for correctly.

Feed the rested dough through the
highest setting first. Do this several times
before gradually reducing the settings until
the dough is of the required thickness.

If you have a special cutter attachment,
use this to produce tagliatelle or fettuccine.

A narrower cutter will produce
spaghetti or tagliarini.

soups & light meals

Adding pasta to soup is not merely a way of "padding it out" to make it go further, although it does, of course, add substance. It is an integral part of the recipe and the soup would not have the same appearance, texture, and balance without it. In Italy, soup is rarely served at lunch and is usually the first course at dinner. The classic recipes here, such as Minestrone Milanese (see page 18), certainly do make wonderful appetizers, but they are also substantial enough to serve as a one-pot meal, perhaps with some fresh bread or rolls, for a light lunch. Pasta is the perfect choice when you are feeling in need of an energy boost, but not hungry enough for a full meal, and many of the recipes here can be prepared and cooked within 15–20 minutes.

As pasta is so versatile, the range of dishes is extensive, from the classic simplicity of Spaghetti Olio e Aglio (see page 51) to the rich creaminess of Pipe Rigate with Gorgonzola Sauce (see page 43); and from the extravagant elegance of Fusilli with Smoked Salmon (see page 39) to the comforting familiarity of Macaroni Cheese Special (see page 42). Whether you are a vegetarian or meat-eater, and whether your preferences are for ham, bacon, cheese, fish, shellfish, herbs, vegetables, mushrooms, or nuts, serve them with pasta for a satisfying snack at any time of day.

brown lentil & pasta soup

serves 4   **prep: 5 mins** 🕐   **cook: 25 mins** 🕓

In Italy, this soup is called Minestrade Lentiche. A "minestra" is a soup cooked with pasta; here, farfalline, a small bow-shaped variety, is used.

INGREDIENTS

4 strips lean bacon,
cut into small squares

1 onion, chopped

2 garlic cloves, crushed

2 celery stalks, chopped

1¾ oz/50 g farfalline or spaghetti,
broken into small pieces

14 oz/400 g canned brown
lentils, drained

5 cups hot Vegetable Stock
(see page 12)

2 tbsp chopped fresh mint

fresh mint sprigs, to garnish

NUTRITIONAL INFORMATION

Calories	.225
Protein	.13g
Carbohydrate	.27g
Sugars	.1g
Fat	.8g
Saturates	.3g

1 Place the bacon in a large skillet together with the onion, garlic, and celery. Dry fry for 4–5 minutes, stirring, until the onion is tender and the bacon is just beginning to brown.

2 Add the pasta to the skillet and cook, stirring, for 1 minute to coat the pasta in the fat.

3 Add the lentils and the Stock, and bring to a boil. Reduce the heat and let simmer for 12–15 minutes, or until the pasta is tender but still firm to the bite.

4 Remove the skillet from the heat and stir in the chopped fresh mint. Transfer the soup to warmed soup bowls, garnish with fresh mint sprigs, and serve immediately.

cook's tip

If you prefer to use dried lentils, add the stock before the pasta and cook for 1–1¼ hours, until the lentils are tender. Add the pasta and cook for a further 12–15 minutes.

chicken & pasta broth

cook: 5 mins   **prep: 15–20 mins**   **serves 6**

This satisfying soup makes a good lunch or supper dish and you can use any vegetables you like. Children will love the tiny pasta shapes. Serve with fresh crusty bread.

NUTRITIONAL INFORMATION	
Calories	185
Protein	17g
Carbohydrate	20g
Sugars	5g
Fat	5g
Saturates	1g

INGREDIENTS

12 oz/350 g boneless chicken breasts

2 tbsp corn oil

1 onion, diced

2 cups carrots, diced

9 oz/250 g cauliflower florets

3½ cups Chicken Stock (see page 12)

2 tsp dried mixed herbs

4½ oz/125 g dried small pasta shapes

salt and pepper

freshly grated Parmesan cheese, for sprinkling (optional)

crusty bread, to serve

cook's tip

You can use any small pasta shapes for this soup—try conchigliette or ditalini or even spaghetti broken up into small pieces. To make a fun soup for children you could add animal-shaped or alphabet pasta.

1 Using a sharp knife, finely dice the chicken, discarding any skin.

2 Heat the corn oil in a large pan and quickly cook the chicken, onion, carrots, and cauliflower until they are lightly colored.

3 Stir in the Chicken Stock and dried mixed herbs, and bring to a boil.

4 Add the pasta shapes to the pan and return to a boil. Cover the pan and let the broth simmer for 10 minutes, stirring occasionally to prevent the pasta sticking together.

5 Season the broth with salt and pepper to taste and sprinkle with grated Parmesan cheese, if using. Serve with fresh crusty bread.

minestrone milanese

serves 6

prep: 20 mins, plus 3 hrs soaking

cook: 1 hr 45 mins

This famous vegetable soup originated in Milan, but there are different versions made throughout Italy and, indeed, across the rest of the world.

INGREDIENTS

2 tbsp olive oil

2 oz/55 g rindless pancetta or lean bacon, diced

2 onions, sliced

2 garlic cloves, finely chopped

3 carrots, chopped

2 celery stalks, chopped

1⅓ cups Great Northern beans, soaked in cold water to cover for 3–4 hours

14 oz/400 g canned chopped tomatoes

scant 8½ cups Beef Stock (see page 12)

12 oz/350 g potatoes, diced

6 oz/175 g dried pepe bucato, macaroni, or other soup pasta shapes

6 oz/175 g green beans, sliced

1 cup fresh or frozen peas

8 oz/225 g savoy cabbage, shredded

3 tbsp chopped fresh flatleaf parsley

salt and pepper

fresh Parmesan cheese shavings, to serve

NUTRITIONAL INFORMATION	
Calories	.380
Protein	.18g
Carbohydrate	.63g
Sugars	.12g
Fat	.8g
Saturates	.2g

cook's tip

It usually takes 1–1½ hours of cooking for soaked Great Northern beans to become tender, but this can vary depending on how long they have been stored.

1 Heat the olive oil in a large heavy-bottom pan. Add the pancetta, onions, and garlic, and cook, stirring occasionally, for 5 minutes. Add the carrots and celery and cook, stirring occasionally, for an additional 5 minutes, or until all the vegetables are softened.

2 Drain the Great Northern beans and add them to the pan with the tomatoes and their can juices and the Beef Stock. Bring to a boil, reduce the heat, cover, and let simmer for 1 hour.

3 Add the potatoes, re-cover and cook for 15 minutes, then add the pasta, green beans, peas, cabbage, and parsley. Cover and cook for an additional 15 minutes, until all the vegetables are tender. Season to taste with salt and pepper. Ladle into warmed soup bowls and serve immediately with Parmesan cheese shavings.

tomato soup with stellete

cook: 1 hr 15 mins   **prep: 10 mins**   **serves 4**

Popular with children and adults, this soup is the perfect choice for a family supper or, served with fresh focaccia, for a light lunch.

INGREDIENTS

2 tbsp olive oil

3 garlic cloves, finely chopped

2 celery stalks, thinly sliced

3 tbsp chopped fresh flatleaf parsley

12 fresh basil leaves, shredded

2 plum tomatoes, peeled, seeded, and diced

scant 1¼ cups strained tomatoes

pinch of cayenne pepper

generous 6⅓ cups Beef or Chicken Stock (see page 12)

salt

6 oz/175 g dried stellete or other soup pasta shapes

fresh basil sprigs, to garnish

freshly grated Parmesan cheese, to serve

variation

If strained tomatoes are unavailable, use 14 oz/400 g canned tomatoes. Rub, with the juice, through a strainer before adding to the pan in Step 1.

cook's tip

Use sun-ripened plum tomatoes, if possible, as they are less watery than ordinary varieties, so are more suitable for using in sauces.

1 Heat the olive oil in a large heavy-bottom pan. Add the garlic, celery, parsley, and basil, and cook, stirring constantly, for 3 minutes. Add the tomatoes and strained tomatoes and season to taste with cayenne pepper. Cook, stirring constantly, for 10 minutes.

2 Pour in the Beef Stock and bring to a boil. Season to taste with salt. Reduce the heat, cover, and let simmer for 45 minutes.

3 Add the pasta and return the soup to a boil. Cook, stirring occasionally, for an additional 10–15 minutes, or until the pasta is just tender. Ladle into warmed soup bowls, garnish with fresh basil sprigs, and serve immediately with the grated Parmesan cheese.

potato & pesto soup

serves 4   **prep: 5–10 mins**   **cook: 45 mins**

Fresh pesto is a treat to the taste buds and very different in flavor from that available from supermarkets. Store the pesto in the refrigerator for up to four days.

INGREDIENTS

3 slices rindless, smoked, fatty bacon
or pancetta

1 lb/450 g mealy potatoes

1 lb/450 g onions

2 tbsp olive oil

2 tbsp butter

2½ cups Chicken Stock (see page 12)

2½ cups milk

3½ oz/100 g dried conchigliette

⅔ cup heavy cream

chopped fresh parsley

salt and pepper

garlic bread, to serve

PESTO SAUCE

2 oz/55 g finely chopped fresh parsley

2 garlic cloves, crushed

½ cup pine nuts, crushed

2 tbsp chopped fresh basil leaves

½ cup freshly grated Parmesan cheese,
plus extra to serve

white pepper

⅔ cup olive oil

NUTRITIONAL INFORMATION

Calories 548

Protein 11g

Carbohydrate 10g

Sugars 0g

Fat 52g

Saturates 18g

variation

To make the classic pesto substitute the parsley with the same amount of fresh basil. Fresh cilantro also makes a good alternative.

1 To make the pesto sauce, put all of the ingredients in a blender or food processor and process for 2 minutes, or blend by hand using a pestle and mortar.

2 Finely chop the bacon, potatoes, and onions. Cook the bacon in a large pan over medium heat for 4 minutes. Add the butter, potatoes, and onions, and cook for 12 minutes, stirring constantly.

3 Add the Stock and milk to the pan, bring to a boil and simmer for 10 minutes. Add the conchigliette and simmer for an additional 10–12 minutes.

cook's tip

When buying onions, always choose ones that feel firm with papery skins and avoid ones that are bruised. Ordinary onions are used in this recipe, but you can use other varieties, if you like.

4 Blend in the cream and simmer for 5 minutes. Add the chopped parsley, salt and pepper to taste, and 2 tablespoons of the pesto sauce. Transfer the soup to individual serving bowls and serve with Parmesan cheese and fresh garlic bread.

tuscan bean soup

serves 6   **prep: 15 mins** ⟳   **cook: 20 mins** ⟳

For a warming meal on a cold winter's day, this filling bean soup will satisfy even the heartiest of appetites.

INGREDIENTS

10½ oz/300 g canned cannellini beans, drained and rinsed
10½ oz/300 g canned cranberry beans, drained and rinsed
about 2½ cups Chicken or Vegetable Stock (see page 12)
4 oz/115 g dried conchigliette or other small pasta shapes
4–5 tbsp olive oil
2 garlic cloves, very finely chopped
3 tbsp chopped fresh flatleaf parsley
salt and pepper

NUTRITIONAL INFORMATION	
Calories	189
Protein	7g
Carbohydrate	24g
Sugars	2g
Fat	8g
Saturates	1g

variation

You can substitute other beans, such as Great Northern or lima beans, for one or both of the beans in the recipe, if you like.

1 Place half the cannellini and half the cranberry beans in a food processor with half the Chicken Stock and process until smooth. Pour into a large heavy-bottom pan and add the remaining beans. Stir in enough of the remaining stock to achieve the consistency you like, then bring to a boil.

2 Add the pasta and return to a boil, then reduce the heat and cook for 15 minutes, or until just tender.

3 Meanwhile, heat 3 tablespoons of the oil in a small skillet. Add the garlic and cook, stirring constantly, for 2–3 minutes, or until golden. Stir the garlic into the soup with the parsley. Season to taste with salt and pepper and ladle into warmed soup bowls. Drizzle with the remaining olive oil to taste and serve immediately.

chicken soup with capelli d'angelo

⏱ **cook: 20 mins**   ⏲ **prep: 5 mins**   **serves 6**

*This unusual version of ever-popular chicken soup is easy to
prepare. Serve with hot, crusty bread for a delicious light meal.*

NUTRITIONAL INFORMATION	
Calories	134
Protein	10g
Carbohydrate	14g
Sugars	1g
Fat	5g
Saturates	1g

INGREDIENTS

generous 6⅓ cups Chicken Stock
(see page 12)
4 oz/115 g skinless, boneless chicken
breast, cut into thin strips
3 eggs
2 tbsp chopped fresh parsley
salt and pepper
corn oil, for brushing
4 oz/115 g dried capelli d'angelo

variation

Use shredded, leftover
cooked chicken instead of
fresh chicken and
substitute the pasta with
other types of soup pasta,
such as anellini or ditali.

1 Bring the Chicken Stock
to a boil in a large
heavy-bottom pan. Add the
chicken strips, reduce
the heat, and let simmer for
10 minutes.

2 Meanwhile, beat the
eggs with the parsley
in a small bowl and season to
taste with salt and pepper.
Brush a small omelet pan with

oil and heat. Add half the egg
mixture, swirl the pan to cover
the bottom evenly, and cook
for 2–3 minutes, or until set.
Slide the omelet out of the pan
and make a second omelet in
the same way.

3 Add the pasta to the
stock in the pan,
return to a boil and cook for
5 minutes, or until the pasta is

nearly tender. Roll up the
omelets and slice thinly.
Add the omelet strips to the
pan and season to taste with
salt and pepper. Heat through
for 1–2 minutes, then ladle
into warmed soup bowls and
serve immediately.

italian chicken soup

serves 4　　　　**prep: 10 mins** 🕐　　　　**cook: 25 mins** 🕐

*This thick, rich soup is an ideal dish for cold, wintry evenings.
It will taste best if it is made with homemade chicken stock.*

INGREDIENTS

1 lb/450 g skinless, boneless chicken
breast, cut into thin strips

5 cups Chicken Stock
(see page 12)

⅔ cup heavy cream or
panna da cucina

salt and pepper

4 oz/115 g dried vermicelli

1 tbsp cornstarch

3 tbsp milk

6 oz/175 g canned corn
kernels, drained

variation

For a chunkier version, you can use
other types of pasta, such as farfalle
(pasta bows), ruotini (little wheels), or
fusilli (spirals).

cook's tip

Always cook pasta in a large
pan with plenty of well salted
water. Once the water has
come to a boil, add the
pasta all at once, and cook,
uncovered, until the pasta is
just tender (al dente).

1 Place the chicken in a
large pan and pour in
the Chicken Stock and cream.
Bring to a boil, then reduce
the heat and let simmer for
20 minutes.

2 Meanwhile, bring a
large heavy-bottom
pan of lightly salted water to
a boil. Add the pasta, return
to a boil, and cook for
10–12 minutes, or until just
tender but still firm to the
bite. Drain the pasta well and
keep warm.

3 Season the soup with
salt and pepper to
taste. Mix the cornstarch and
milk together until a smooth
paste forms, then stir it into
the soup. Add the corn and
pasta and heat through. Ladle
the soup into warmed soup
bowls and serve.

fish soup with anellini

serves 6   **prep: 15 mins**   **cook: 30 mins**

This hearty combination of fish, shellfish, tomatoes, and pasta is more of a stew than a soup and would make a very filling and nutritious one-pot meal served with French bread.

INGREDIENTS

2 tbsp olive oil

2 onions, sliced

1 garlic clove, finely chopped

4 cups Fish Stock

(see page 12) or water

14 oz/400 g canned chopped tomatoes

¼ tsp herbes de Provence

¼ tsp saffron threads

4 oz/115 g dried anellini

salt and pepper

1 lb/450 g angler fish fillet, cut into chunks

18 live mussels, scrubbed and debearded (see Cook's Tip)

8 oz/225 g raw shrimp, shelled and deveined, tails left on

NUTRITIONAL INFORMATION

Calories 236

Protein 28g

Carbohydrate 20g

Sugars 5g

Fat 6g

Saturates 1g

variation

Other types of fish would also work well in this dish. Try cod or fresh haddock instead of the angler fish, if you prefer.

cook's tip

Buy a few more live mussels than you need for this recipe. Before you start cooking, discard any with broken shells, or any that refuse to close when tapped with a knife.

1 Heat the olive oil in a large heavy-bottom pan. Add the onions and garlic and cook over low heat, stirring occasionally, for 5 minutes, or until the onions have softened.

2 Add the Fish Stock with the tomatoes and their can juices, herbs, saffron, and pasta, and season to taste with salt and pepper. Bring to a boil, then cover and let simmer for 15 minutes.

3 Add the fish, mussels, and shrimp. Re-cover the pan and let simmer for an additional 5–10 minutes, until the mussels have opened, the shrimp have changed color, and the fish is opaque and flakes easily. Discard any mussels that remain closed. Ladle the soup into warmed bowls and serve.

vegetable & bean soup

serves 4   **prep: 30 mins** ⏱   **cook: 30 mins** ⏱

This wonderful combination of cannellini beans, vegetables, and vermicelli is made even richer by the addition of homemade pesto and dried mushrooms.

INGREDIENTS

1 small eggplant

2 large tomatoes

1 potato, peeled

1 carrot

1 leek

425 g/15 oz canned cannellini beans

3½ cups hot Vegetable or Chicken Stock (see page 12)

2 tsp dried basil

½ oz/15 g dried porcini mushrooms, soaked for 10 minutes in enough warm water to cover

1¾ oz/50 g vermicelli

3 tbsp Pesto (see page 46 or use store bought)

freshly grated Parmesan cheese, to serve (optional)

variation

Replace the cannellini beans with either canned kidney beans or mixed beans, if you prefer.

cook's tip

If you don't have time to make pesto, then use a store-bought one. Pesto is available in most supermarkets. Once opened, cover the remaining pesto with a little olive oil and store in the refrigerator for up to 14 days.

1 Slice the eggplant into rings about ½-inch/1-cm thick, then cut each ring into 4. Cut the tomatoes and potato into small dice. Cut the carrot into sticks, about 1-inch/2.5-cm long, and cut the leek into rings.

2 Place the cannellini beans and their liquid in a large pan. Add the eggplant, tomatoes, potatoes, carrot, and leek, stirring to mix.

3 Add the Stock to the pan and bring to a boil. Reduce the heat and let simmer for 15 minutes. Add the basil, dried mushrooms and their soaking liquid, and the vermicelli, and simmer for 5 minutes, or until all of the vegetables are tender. Remove the pan from the heat and stir in the Pesto. Serve with freshly grated Parmesan cheese, if using.

mussel soup

serves 4   **prep: 15 mins**   **cook: 35–40 mins**

Thick, creamy and full of flavor, this is a fabulous soup for cheering you up on a cold winter's day. Serve with crusty bread.

INGREDIENTS

1 lb 10 oz/750 g mussels, scrubbed and debearded (see Cook's Tip)

2 tbsp olive oil

salt and pepper

3½ oz/100 g butter

1 onion, chopped

2 garlic cloves, finely chopped

2 oz/55 g rindless lean bacon, chopped

⅜ cup all-purpose flour

3 potatoes, thinly sliced

4 oz/115 g dried farfalle

1¼ cups heavy cream or panna da cucina

1 tbsp lemon juice

2 egg yolks

2 tbsp finely chopped fresh parsley, to garnish

NUTRITIONAL INFORMATION	
Calories	.933
Protein	.23g
Carbohydrate	.57g
Sugars	.6g
Fat	.70g
Saturates	.39g

variation

Substitute the rindless lean bacon with the same amount of pancetta and replace the dried farfalle with either fusilli or conchiglie, if you like.

cook's tip

To prepare mussels, scrub or scrape the shells and pull out any beards that are attached to them. Discard any with broken shells or that refuse to close when tapped with a knife.

1 Bring a large heavy-bottom pan of water to a boil. Add the mussels and olive oil and season to taste with pepper. Cover tightly and cook over high heat for 5 minutes, or until the mussels have opened. Remove the mussels with a slotted spoon, discarding any that remain closed. Strain the cooking liquid and set aside 5 cups.

Remove the mussels from their shells and set aside until required.

2 Melt the butter in a clean pan. Add the bacon, onion, and garlic, and cook over low heat, stirring occasionally, for 5 minutes. Stir in the flour and cook, stirring, for 1 minute. Gradually stir in all but 2 tablespoons of the

reserved cooking liquid and bring to a boil, stirring constantly. Add the potato slices and let simmer for 5 minutes. Add the pasta and let simmer for an additional 10 minutes.

3 Stir in the cream and lemon juice and season to taste with salt and pepper. Add the mussels. Mix the egg

yolks and the remaining mussel cooking liquid together, then stir the mixture into the soup and cook for 4 minutes, until thickened.

4 Ladle the soup into warmed soup bowls, garnish with chopped parsley, and serve immediately.

spaghetti alla puttanesca

serves 4   **prep: 10 mins** ⏲   **cook: 35–40 mins** ⏲

Simplicity itself, this speedy pantry dish makes a really tasty lunch or light supper when you are in a hurry.

INGREDIENTS

3 tbsp olive oil

2 garlic cloves, finely chopped

10 canned anchovy fillets, drained and chopped

scant 1 cup black olives, pitted and chopped

1 tbsp capers, drained and rinsed

1 lb/450 g plum tomatoes, peeled, seeded, and chopped

pinch of cayenne pepper

salt

14 oz/400 g dried spaghetti

2 tbsp chopped fresh parsley, to garnish (optional)

NUTRITIONAL INFORMATION

Calories	.485
Protein	.15g
Carbohydrate	.78g
Sugars	.7g
Fat	.15g
Saturates	.2g

variation

You can substitute 14 oz/ 400 g canned chopped tomatoes and their can juices for the fresh tomatoes, if you prefer.

1 Heat the olive oil in a heavy-bottom skillet. Add the garlic and cook over low heat, stirring frequently, for 2 minutes. Add the anchovies and mash them to a pulp with a fork. Add the olives, capers, and tomatoes, and season to taste with cayenne pepper. Cover and let simmer for 25 minutes.

2 Meanwhile, bring a large heavy-bottom pan of lightly salted water to a boil. Add the pasta, return to a boil, and cook for 8–10 minutes, or until tender but still firm to the bite. Drain well and transfer to a warmed serving dish.

3 Spoon the anchovy sauce into the dish and toss the pasta, using 2 large forks. Garnish with the chopped parsley, if using, and serve immediately.

pasta with prosciutto

cook: 15 mins   **prep: 10 mins**   **serves 4**

Rich and subtle in flavor and very quick to prepare, this dish would make an excellent choice for an informal dinner party.

NUTRITIONAL INFORMATION	
Calories	700
Protein	25g
Carbohydrate	65g
Sugars	6g
Fat	38g
Saturates	23g

INGREDIENTS

4 oz/115 g prosciutto

4 tbsp unsalted butter

1 small onion, finely chopped

salt and pepper

12 oz/350 g dried green and
white tagliatelle

⅔ cup heavy cream or
panna da cucina

½ cup freshly grated
Parmesan cheese

cook's tip

Prosciutto is an Italian dry-cured ham. The best-known variety is Parma ham, but other areas produce their own types. *Prosciutto di San Daniele* is strong, while hams from Veneto have a delicate flavor.

1 Trim off the fat from the prosciutto, then finely chop both the fat and the lean meat, keeping them separate. Melt the butter in a heavy-bottom skillet. Add the prosciutto fat and onion and cook over low heat, stirring occasionally, for 10 minutes.

2 Meanwhile, bring a large heavy-bottom pan of lightly salted water to a boil. Add the pasta, return to a boil, and cook for 8–10 minutes, or until tender but still firm to the bite.

3 Add the lean prosciutto to the skillet and cook, stirring occasionally, for

2 minutes. Stir in the cream, then season to taste with pepper and heat through gently. Drain the pasta and transfer to a warmed serving dish. Add the prosciutto mixture and toss well, then stir in the grated Parmesan cheese. Serve immediately.

paglia e fieno with garlic crumbs

serves 4 **prep: 10 mins** **cook: 10 mins**

*This tasty, classic combination of pasta, pine nuts, and cheese
is incredibly easy to make and is ideal if you are in a hurry.*

INGREDIENTS

6 cups fresh white bread crumbs

4 tbsp finely chopped fresh
flatleaf parsley

1 tbsp chopped fresh chives

2 tbsp finely chopped fresh
sweet marjoram

3 tbsp olive oil, plus extra to serve

3–4 garlic cloves, finely chopped

½ cup pine nuts

salt and pepper

1 lb/450 g fresh paglia e fieno

½ cup freshly grated
pecorino cheese, to serve

NUTRITIONAL INFORMATION	
Calories	.788
Protein	.27g
Carbohydrate	.113g
Sugars	.6g
Fat	.28g
Saturates	.5g

variation

For a spicy version of this dish, add
1–2 teaspoons crushed, dried chiles to
the bread crumb mixture in Step 1.

cook's tip

Pecorino cheese is an Italian
hard cheese, made from ewe's
milk. Pecorino Romano, from
central and southern Italy, is
widely available. Other varieties
include Peperino Sardo and
Sardo extra mature.

1 Mix the bread crumbs, parsley, chives, and marjoram together in a small bowl. Heat the olive oil in a large heavy-bottom skillet. Add the bread crumb mixture and the garlic and pine nuts, season to taste with salt and pepper, and cook over low heat, stirring constantly, for 5 minutes, or until the bread crumbs become golden, but

not crisp. Remove the skillet from the heat and cover to keep warm.

2 Bring a large heavy-bottom pan of lightly salted water to a boil. Add the pasta, return to a boil, and cook for 4–5 minutes, or until tender but still firm to the bite.

3 Drain the pasta and transfer to a warmed serving dish. Drizzle with 2–3 tablespoons of olive oil and toss to mix. Add the garlic bread crumbs and toss again. Serve immediately with the grated pecorino cheese.

spaghetti alla carbonara

serves 4 | **prep: 10 mins** | **cook: 10 mins**

The trick is to keep everything hot, so that when you add the eggs at the end, they just cook in the residual heat, but do not scramble.

INGREDIENTS

1 lb/450 g dried spaghetti

1 tbsp olive oil

8 oz/225 g rindless pancetta or lean bacon, chopped

4 eggs

5 tbsp light cream

salt and pepper

2 tbsp freshly grated Parmesan cheese

NUTRITIONAL INFORMATION

Calories 709

Protein 32g

Carbohydrate 84g

Sugars 5g

Fat 30g

Saturates 10g

variation

For a more substantial dish, cook 1–2 finely chopped shallots with the pancetta and add 2 cups sliced mushrooms after 4 minutes.

1 Bring a large heavy-bottom pan of lightly salted water to a boil. Add the pasta, return to a boil, and cook for 8–10 minutes, or until tender but still firm to the bite.

2 Meanwhile, heat the olive oil in a heavy-bottom skillet. Add the pancetta strips and cook over medium heat, stirring frequently, for 8–10 minutes.

3 Beat the eggs with the cream in a small bowl and season to taste with salt and pepper. Drain the pasta and return it to the pan. Tip in the contents of the skillet, then add the egg mixture and half the Parmesan cheese. Stir well, then transfer to a warmed serving dish. Serve immediately, sprinkled with the remaining cheese.

fusilli with smoked salmon

cook: 10–12 mins　　　　**prep: 10 mins**　　　　**serves 4**

This simple dish provides a taste of luxury that is irresistible. Serve as an appetizer or add a salad to make a main course.

NUTRITIONAL INFORMATION

Calories 1064

Protein 30g

Carbohydrate 88g

Sugars 8g

Fat 67g

Saturates 40g

INGREDIENTS

1 lb/450 g dried fusilli

4 tbsp unsalted butter

1 small onion, finely chopped

6 tbsp dry white wine

scant 2 cups heavy cream

salt and pepper

8 oz/225 g smoked salmon

2 tbsp chopped fresh dill

1–2 tbsp lemon juice

TO GARNISH

½ lemon

fresh dill sprig

cook's tip

Smoked salmon offcuts and misshapen pieces are much less expensive than slices and work perfectly well in this dish.

1 Bring a large heavy-bottom pan of lightly salted water to a boil. Add the pasta, return to a boil, and cook for 8–10 minutes, or until tender but still firm to the bite.

2 Meanwhile, melt the butter in a heavy-bottom pan. Add the onion and cook over low heat, stirring occasionally, for 5 minutes, or until softened. Add the wine, bring to a boil and continue boiling until reduced by two-thirds. Pour in the cream and season to taste with salt and pepper. Bring to a boil, reduce the heat, and let simmer for 2 minutes, or until slightly thickened. Cut the smoked salmon into squares and stir into the pan with the dill and lemon juice to taste.

3 Drain the pasta and transfer to a warmed serving dish. Add the smoked salmon mixture and toss well. Cut the top part of the rind of the lemon half into a spiral shape, and place the lemon half on top of the pasta to garnish. Add a dill sprig and serve.

spicy mushroom pasta

⏲ **cook: 1 hr 15 mins**   ⏱ **prep: 10 mins**   **serves 4**

variation

If you prefer a milder flavor, reduce the number of chiles. Alternatively, omit Step 2 completely and serve the penne with the mushroom sauce.

This richly flavored sauce would go very well with any type of short pasta, such as fusilli, conchiglie, or even orecchiette.

INGREDIENTS

1 tbsp butter

6 tbsp olive oil

8 oz/225 g exotic mushrooms, sliced

scant ¼ cup all-purpose flour

generous ¾ cup Beef Stock (see page 12)

⅔ cup full-bodied red wine

4 tomatoes, peeled and chopped

1 tbsp tomato paste

1 tsp sugar

1 tbsp shredded fresh basil

salt and pepper

2 garlic cloves, finely chopped

2 fresh red chiles, seeded and chopped

2 fresh green chiles, seeded and chopped

14 oz/400 g dried penne

cook's tip

Do not overdrain pasta, as some of the starch that is left will help the sauce stick to the pasta. Alternatively, set aside 1–2 tablespoons of the pasta cooking water and stir it in before adding the sauce.

1 Melt the butter and 4 tablespoons of the olive oil in a large heavy-bottom pan. Add the mushrooms and cook over medium heat, stirring occasionally, for 5 minutes. Stir in the flour and cook, stirring constantly, for 1 minute. Gradually stir in the Beef Stock and wine, bring to a boil, reduce the heat, and let simmer for 15 minutes. Add

the tomatoes, tomato paste, sugar, and basil, season to taste with salt and pepper and let simmer for an additional 30 minutes.

2 Heat the remaining olive oil in a large skillet. Add the garlic and chiles and cook, stirring constantly, for 5 minutes. Stir in the mushroom mixture, taste

and adjust the seasoning, if necessary, then let simmer over low heat for 20 minutes.

3 Meanwhile, bring a large heavy-bottom pan of lightly salted water to a boil. Add the pasta, return to a boil, and cook for 8–10 minutes, or until tender but still firm to the bite.

4 Drain the pasta and transfer to a warmed serving dish. Add the spicy mushroom sauce, toss well, and serve immediately.

macaroni cheese special

serves 4   **prep: 10 mins** ⌛   **cook: 20 mins** ⌛

This version of the family favorite is always popular with children and makes the perfect weekend lunch dish.

INGREDIENTS

salt

8 oz/225 g dried short-cut macaroni

8 frankfurters

7 oz/200 g canned corn, drained

3 scallions, thinly sliced

CHEESE SAUCE

3 tbsp butter

generous ¼ cup all-purpose flour

scant 2 cups milk

salt and pepper

1 tbsp Dijon mustard

6 oz/175 g Cheddar cheese, grated

4 oz/115 g Gruyère cheese, grated

NUTRITIONAL INFORMATION

Calories 898

Protein 39g

Carbohydrate 70g

Sugars 12g

Fat 53g

Saturates 26g

variation

This dish would also work well with other dried short pasta shapes, such as rotelle, penne, fusilli bucati, or even eliche (spirals).

1 Bring a large heavy-bottom pan of lightly salted water to a boil. Add the macaroni, return to a boil, and cook for 8–10 minutes, or until tender but still firm to the bite. Meanwhile, cook the frankfurters in boiling water or in the microwave according to the package instructions. Drain the macaroni and place in a large heatproof bowl,

then cut the frankfurters into thick slices and stir them into the macaroni.

2 To make the sauce, melt the butter in a small pan. Add the flour and cook, stirring constantly, for 1 minute. Gradually stir in the milk, then bring to a boil, stirring constantly. Cook, stirring, for 1–2 minutes, or

until thickened, then remove from the heat, season to taste with salt and pepper, and stir in the mustard, Gruyère cheese, and 1 cup of the Cheddar cheese.

3 Stir the corn and scallions into the macaroni, then fold in the sauce. Sprinkle the remaining grated Cheddar cheese

evenly over the top and cook under a preheated hot broiler for 2–3 minutes, or until the topping is golden and bubbling. Serve immediately.

pipe rigate with gorgonzola sauce

cook: 12–15 mins   **prep: 5 mins**   **serves 4**

This is a very rich-tasting sauce, so a little of this dish goes a long way. It would make a good appetizer for an informal lunch party.

NUTRITIONAL INFORMATION	
Calories	.770
Protein	.23g
Carbohydrate	.78g
Sugars	.4g
Fat	.43g
Saturates	.26g

INGREDIENTS

14 oz/400 g dried pipe rigate

2 tbsp unsalted butter

6 fresh sage leaves

7 oz/200 g Gorgonzola cheese, diced

¾–1 cup heavy cream or

panna da cucina

2 tbsp dry vermouth

salt and pepper

cook's tip

Gorgonzola should be creamy colored with pale green marbling and a pleasant aroma. Do not buy it if it is hard, discolored, or smelly.

1 Bring a large heavy-bottom pan of lightly salted water to a boil. Add the pasta, return to a boil, and cook for 8–10 minutes, until tender but still firm to the bite.

2 Meanwhile, melt the butter in a separate heavy-bottom pan. Add the sage leaves and cook, stirring gently, for 1 minute. Remove and set aside the sage leaves. Add the cheese and cook, stirring constantly, over low heat until it has melted. Gradually, stir in ¾ cup of the cream and the vermouth. Season to taste with salt and pepper and cook, stirring, until thickened. Add more cream if the sauce seems too thick.

3 Drain the pasta well and transfer to a warmed serving dish. Add the Gorgonzola sauce, toss well to mix, and serve immediately, garnished with the reserved sage leaves.

fettuccine with ricotta

serves 4   **prep: 10 mins**   **cook: 10 mins**

Very little cooking is involved in the preparation of this lovely, light pasta dish, so it makes an excellent choice for a light lunch in hot weather, served with mixed salad greens.

INGREDIENTS

12 oz/350 g dried fettuccine

3 tbsp unsalted butter

2 tbsp chopped fresh
flatleaf parsley

generous ½ cup ricotta cheese

generous 1 cup ground almonds

⅔ cup sour cream

2 tbsp extra virgin olive oil

½ cup hot Chicken Stock
(see page 12)

pinch of freshly grated nutmeg

salt and pepper

1 tbsp pine nuts

fresh flatleaf parsley leaves,
to garnish

NUTRITIONAL INFORMATION

Calories 730

Protein 21g

Carbohydrate 70g

Sugars 5g

Fat 43g

Saturates 14g

variation

To give a sharp, piquant flavor to the sauce, add the finely grated rind and juice of ½ lemon with the ground almonds in Step 2.

cook's tip

It is important that you mix the ricotta, ground almonds, and sour cream into a smooth paste before adding the oil in Step 2. Equally, don't add the stock until the oil has been completely absorbed.

1 Bring a large heavy-bottom pan of lightly salted water to a boil. Add the pasta, return to a boil, and cook for 8–10 minutes, or until tender but still firm to the bite. Drain well and return to the pan. Add the butter and chopped parsley and toss thoroughly to coat.

2 Mix the ricotta, ground almonds, and sour cream together in a bowl. Gradually stir in the olive oil, followed by the hot Chicken Stock. Season to taste with nutmeg and pepper.

3 Transfer the pasta to a warmed dish, pour over the sauce, and toss. Sprinkle with pine nuts, garnish with parsley leaves, and serve immediately.

pasta with pesto

serves 4   prep: 15 mins   cook: 8–10 mins

Homemade pesto is much more delicious than even good-quality, store-bought brands and it makes a wonderful nocook sauce for all types of freshly cooked pasta.

INGREDIENTS

¾ cup fresh basil leaves

½ cup pine nuts

4 garlic cloves, coarsely chopped

salt

2 cups freshly grated
Parmesan cheese

1 cup extra virgin olive oil

1 lb/450 g dried spaghetti

fresh basil sprigs, to garnish (optional)

NUTRITIONAL INFORMATION

Calories	.1124
Protein	.39g
Carbohydrate	.87g
Sugars	.4g
Fat	.71g
Saturates	.18g

cook's tip

If you want to make the pesto in advance, store it, covered with a thin layer of olive oil, in a screw-top jar in the refrigerator. It can be stored in the refrigerator for 3–4 days

1 Place the basil leaves, pine nuts, and garlic in a large mortar and add a generous pinch of salt. Grind to a paste with a pestle. Gradually work in the Parmesan cheese until the mixture is smooth. Add the olive oil in a slow trickle, beating constantly with a wooden spoon, then set aside until required.

2 Bring a large heavy-bottom pan of lightly salted water to a boil. Add the pasta, return to a boil, and cook for 8–10 minutes, or until tender but still firm to the bite.

3 Drain the pasta and set aside 1–2 tablespoons of the cooking water. If you like, thin the pesto slightly with the cooking water, then add to the pasta and toss well. Serve immediately, garnished with basil, if you like.

tagliatelle with walnuts

cook: 8–10 mins   **prep: 10 mins**   **serves 4**

This unusual combination would make an intriguing appetizer for a dinner party, but is also great for a light lunch, if served with a crisp green salad and crusty bread.

NUTRITIONAL INFORMATION	
Calories	1124
Protein	27g
Carbohydrate	75g
Sugars	9g
Fat	82g
Saturates	12g

INGREDIENTS

½ cup fresh white bread crumbs

3 cups walnut pieces

2 garlic cloves, finely chopped

4 tbsp milk

4 tbsp olive oil

⅜ cup cream cheese

⅔ cup light cream

salt and pepper

12 oz/350 g dried tagliatelle

1 Place the bread crumbs, walnuts, garlic, milk, olive oil, and cream cheese in a large mortar and grind to a smooth paste. Alternatively, place the ingredients in a food processor and process until smooth. Stir in the cream to give a thick sauce consistency and season to taste with salt and pepper. Set aside.

2 Bring a large heavy-bottom pan of lightly salted water to a boil. Add the pasta, return to a boil, and cook for 8–10 minutes, or until tender but still firm to the bite.

3 Drain the pasta and transfer to a warmed serving dish. Add the walnut sauce and toss thoroughly to coat. Serve immediately.

cook's tip

You may not need all of the walnut sauce as it is very rich. Store any leftover sauce in a screw-top jar in the refrigerator for up to 2 days.

chorizo & mushroom pasta

serves 6   **prep: 5 mins**   **cook: 20 mins**

Simple and quick to make, this spicy dish is sure to set the taste buds tingling. Delicious served with warm crusty bread and salad for a filling lunch.

INGREDIENTS

1 lb 8 oz/680 g dried vermicelli

½ cup olive oil

2 garlic cloves

4½ oz/125 g chorizo, sliced

8 oz/225 g exotic mushrooms

3 fresh red chiles, chopped

2 tbsp fresh Parmesan cheese shavings, for sprinkling

salt and pepper

10 anchovy fillets, to garnish

NUTRITIONAL INFORMATION

Calories	.495
Protein	.15g
Carbohydrate	.33g
Sugars	.1g
Fat	.35g
Saturates	.5g

variation

Use other types of pasta, such as spaghetti, if you prefer. If you don't like it too spicy, then seed the chiles before using.

cook's tip

Many varieties of mushrooms are cultivated and indistinguishable from the wild varieties. Oyster mushrooms are used here, but you could also use chanterelles. Chanterelles shrink during cooking, so you may need more.

1 Bring a large, heavy-bottom pan of lightly salted water to a boil. Add the vermicelli, return to a boil and cook for 8–10 minutes, or until just tender, but still firm to the bite. Drain the pasta thoroughly, then place on a large, warmed serving plate and keep warm.

2 Meanwhile, heat the olive oil in a skillet. Add the garlic and cook for 1 minute. Add the chorizo and exotic mushrooms and cook for 4 minutes. Add the chopped chiles and cook for an additional 1 minute.

3 Pour the chorizo and exotic mushroom mixture over the vermicelli and season to taste with salt and pepper. Sprinkle with fresh Parmesan cheese shavings, garnish with a lattice of anchovy fillets, and serve immediately.

saffron linguine

Simple and colorful, this delightful dish is perfect for both family suppers and informal entertaining.

INGREDIENTS

12 oz/350 g dried linguine

pinch of saffron threads

2 tbsp water

5 oz/140 g ham, cut into strips

¾ cup heavy cream or panna da cucina

½ cup freshly grated Parmesan cheese

salt and pepper

2 egg yolks

NUTRITIONAL INFORMATION	
Calories	.626
Protein	.25g
Carbohydrate	.66g
Sugars	.4g
Fat	.31g
Saturates	.17g

variation

Replace the ham with the same amount of pancetta or rindless, lean bacon, cut into strips. For a special occasion, use prosciutto.

1 Bring a large heavy-bottom pan of lightly salted water to a boil. Add the pasta, return to a boil, and cook for 8–10 minutes, or until tender but still firm to the bite.

2 Meanwhile, place the saffron in a separate heavy-bottom pan and add the water. Bring to a boil, then remove from the heat and let stand for 5 minutes.

3 Stir the ham, cream, and grated Parmesan cheese into the saffron and return the pan to the heat. Season to taste with salt and pepper and heat through gently, stirring constantly, until simmering. Remove the pan from the heat and beat in the egg yolks. Drain the pasta and transfer to a large, warmed serving dish. Add the saffron sauce, toss well, and serve.

spaghetti olio e aglio

cook: 10 mins   **prep: 5 mins**   **serves 4**

This famous Roman recipe is probably the simplest pasta dish in the world—spaghetti with olive oil and garlic.

NUTRITIONAL INFORMATION	
Calories	.600
Protein	.14g
Carbohydrate	.84g
Sugars	.4g
Fat	.26g
Saturates	.3g

INGREDIENTS

1 lb/450 g dried spaghetti

½ cup extra virgin olive oil

3 garlic cloves, finely chopped

3 tbsp chopped fresh

flatleaf parsley

salt and pepper

cook's tip

Cooked pasta gets cold quickly, so make sure that the serving dish is warmed thoroughly. As soon as the pasta is drained, transfer to the dish, pour over the garlic-flavored olive oil, toss, and serve.

1 Bring a large heavy-bottom pan of lightly salted water to a boil. Add the pasta, return to a boil, and cook for 8–10 minutes, or until tender but still firm to the bite.

2 Meanwhile, heat the olive oil in a heavy-bottom skillet. Add the garlic and a pinch of salt and cook over low heat, stirring constantly, for 3–4 minutes, or until golden. Do not let the garlic brown or it will taste bitter. Remove the skillet from the heat.

3 Drain the pasta and transfer to a large, warmed serving dish. Pour in the garlic-flavored olive oil, then add the chopped parsley and season to taste with salt and pepper. Toss well and serve immediately.

eggplant & pasta

serves 4 **prep: 15 mins plus 12 hrs marinating** **cook: 20 mins**

Prepare the marinated eggplants well in advance so that all you have to do is cook the pasta.

INGREDIENTS

⅔ cup Vegetable Stock
(see page 12)

⅔ cup white wine vinegar

2 tsp balsamic vinegar

3 tbsp olive oil

1 fresh oregano sprig

1 lb/450 g eggplants, peeled
and thinly sliced

14 oz/400 g dried linguine

MARINADE

2 tbsp extra virgin olive oil

2 garlic cloves, crushed

2 tbsp chopped fresh oregano

2 tbsp finely chopped roasted almonds

2 tbsp diced red pepper

2 tbsp lime juice

grated rind and juice of 1 orange

salt and pepper

NUTRITIONAL INFORMATION

Calories	.378
Protein	.12g
Carbohydrate	.16g
Sugars	.3g
Fat	.30g
Saturates	.3g

variation

If you prefer, you can use fresh basil and lemon juice instead of oregano and lime juice in the marinade.

1 Place the Vegetable Stock, wine vinegar, and balsamic vinegar into a large, heavy-bottom pan and bring to a boil over low heat. Add 2 teaspoons of the olive oil and the oregano sprig, and simmer gently for 1 minute. Add the eggplant slices to the pan, remove from the heat and let stand for 10 minutes.

2 Meanwhile make the marinade. Mix the olive oil, garlic, fresh oregano, almonds, pepper, lime juice, orange rind and juice together in a large bowl, and season to taste with salt and pepper.

3 Carefully remove the eggplant from the pan with a slotted spoon, and drain well. Add the eggplant slices to

the marinade, mixing well, and let stand to marinate in the refrigerator for 12 hours.

4 Bring a large, heavy-bottom pan of lightly salted water to a boil. Add half of the remaining olive oil and the linguine, return to a boil, and cook for 8–10 minutes, or until just tender but still firm to the bite.

cook's tip

Balsamic vinegar originates in Modena in Italy. It has a sweet nutty flavor and should be used sparingly. Add toward the end of cooking or heat gently so that none of the flavor is lost.

Drain the pasta thoroughly and toss with the remaining olive oil while still warm. Arrange the pasta on a serving plate with the eggplant slices and the marinade. Serve immediately.

tagliarini all'alfredo

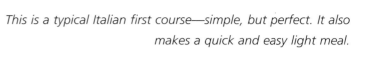

serves 4　　　　prep: 5 mins ⌛　　　　cook: 8–10 mins ⏲

This is a typical Italian first course—simple, but perfect. It also makes a quick and easy light meal.

INGREDIENTS

1 lb/450 g dried tagliarini

2 tbsp unsalted butter

scant 1 cup heavy cream or panna da cucina

½ cup freshly grated Parmesan cheese, plus extra to garnish

pinch of freshly grated nutmeg

salt and pepper

NUTRITIONAL INFORMATION

Calories	.720
Protein	.20g
Carbohydrate	.85g
Sugars	.5g
Fat	.36g
Saturates	.22g

1 Bring a large heavy-bottom pan of lightly salted water to a boil. Add the pasta, return to a boil and cook for 8–10 minutes, or until tender but still firm to the bite.

2 Meanwhile, melt the butter in a separate heavy-bottom pan. Stir in ⅔ cup of the cream, bring to a boil, then reduce the heat and let simmer for 1 minute, until the mixture is slightly thickened.

3 Drain the pasta, then tip it into the butter and cream mixture and stir well to coat. Add the remaining cream and the grated Parmesan cheese. Season to taste with nutmeg, salt, and pepper, and stir. Serve garnished with extra grated Parmesan cheese.

variation

For a more substantial dish, cook 3 cups fresh or frozen peas in the butter for 3 minutes before adding the cream.

pasta with bacon & tomatoes

⏱ **cook: 10 mins** ⏲ **prep: 35 mins** **serves 4**

As this dish cooks, the mouthwatering aroma of bacon, sweet tomatoes, and oregano is a feast in itself.

NUTRITIONAL INFORMATION

Calories 431

Protein 10g

Carbohydrate 34g

Sugars 8g

Fat 29g

Saturates 14g

INGREDIENTS

2 lb/900 g small, sweet tomatoes

6 slices rindless smoked bacon

2 oz/55 g butter

1 onion, chopped

1 garlic clove, crushed

4 fresh oregano sprigs, finely chopped

salt and pepper

1 lb/450 g dried orecchiette

1 tbsp olive oil

freshly grated romano cheese, to serve

cook's tip

For an authentic Italian flavor use pancetta, rather than ordinary bacon. This kind of bacon is streaked with fat and adds flavor to traditional dishes. It is available smoked and unsmoked.

1 Blanch the tomatoes in boiling water. Drain, peel and seed the tomatoes, then coarsely chop the flesh.

2 Using a sharp knife, chop the bacon into small dice. Melt the butter in a pan. Add the bacon and cook until it is golden.

3 Add the onion and garlic, and cook over medium heat for 5–7 minutes, until just softened.

4 Add the tomatoes and oregano to the pan, and then season to taste with salt and pepper. Lower the heat and let simmer for 10–12 minutes.

5 Bring a large pan of lightly salted water to a boil. Add the pasta and oil and cook for 12 minutes, until just tender, but still firm to the bite. Drain the pasta and transfer to a warmed serving dish or bowl.

6 Spoon the bacon and tomato sauce over the pasta, toss to coat, and serve with the romano cheese.

spaghetti with ricotta

serves 4　　　　**prep: 5–10 mins**　　　　**cook: 20 mins**

This light pasta dish has a delicate flavor ideally suited for a summer lunch. Use other types of long pasta, if you prefer.

INGREDIENTS

12 oz/350 g dried spaghetti

3 tbsp butter

2 tbsp chopped fresh flatleaf parsley

1⅓ cups freshly ground almonds

generous ½ cup ricotta cheese

pinch of grated nutmeg

pinch of ground cinnamon

⅔ cup sour cream or yogurt

3 tbsp olive oil

½ cup hot Chicken Stock (see page 12)

1 tbsp pine nuts

salt and pepper

fresh flatleaf parsley sprigs, to garnish

NUTRITIONAL INFORMATION

Calories 701

Protein 17g

Carbohydrate 73g

Sugars 12g

Fat 40g

Saturates 15g

variation

For a vegetarian alternative, use Vegetable Stock (see page 12) instead of the Chicken Stock.

cook's tip

Use 2 large forks to toss spaghetti or other long pasta, so that it is thoroughly coated with the sauce. Special spaghetti forks are available from some cookware departments and kitchen stores.

1 Bring a large, heavy-bottom pan of lightly salted water to a boil. Add the spaghetti, return to a boil and cook for 8–10 minutes, or until tender, but still firm to the bite.

2 Drain the pasta, return to the pan and toss with the butter and chopped parsley. Keep warm.

3 To make the sauce, mix the ground almonds, ricotta cheese, nutmeg, cinnamon, and sour cream or yogurt together in a small pan over low heat to form a thick paste. Gradually stir in the olive oil. When the oil has been fully incorporated, gradually stir in the hot Chicken Stock, until the sauce is smooth. Season to taste with pepper.

4 Transfer the spaghetti to a warmed serving dish, pour over the sauce, and toss together well (see Cook's Tip). Sprinkle over the pine nuts, garnish with the flatleaf parsley sprigs and serve warm.

spinach & anchovy pasta

serves 4 **prep: 10 mins** ⏱ **cook: 25 mins** ⏱

This colorful light meal can be made with a variety of different pasta, including spaghetti and linguine.

INGREDIENTS

2 lb/900 g fresh, young spinach leaves

salt

14 oz/400 g dried fettuccine

5 tbsp olive oil

3 tbsp pine nuts

3 garlic cloves, crushed

8 canned anchovy fillets, drained and chopped

NUTRITIONAL INFORMATION

Calories	.619
Protein	.21g
Carbohydrate	.67g
Sugars	.5g
Fat	.31g
Saturates	.3g

1 Trim off any tough spinach stalks. Rinse the spinach leaves under cold running water and place them in a large pan with only the water that is clinging to them after washing. Cover and cook over high heat, shaking the pan from time to time, until the spinach has wilted, but retains its color. Drain well, set aside, and keep warm.

2 Bring a large heavy-bottom pan of lightly salted water to a boil. Add the fettuccine, return to a boil and cook for 8–10 minutes, or until it is just tender but still firm to the bite.

3 Heat 4 tablespoons of the olive oil in a separate pan. Add the pine nuts and cook until golden.

Remove the pine nuts from the pan and set aside until required.

4 Add the garlic to the pan and cook until golden. Add the anchovies and stir in the spinach. Cook, stirring, for 2–3 minutes, until heated through. Return the pine nuts to the pan.

cook's tip

If you are in a hurry, you can use frozen spinach. Thaw and drain it thoroughly, pressing out as much moisture as possible. Cut the leaves into strips and add to the dish with the anchovies in Step 4.

5 Drain the fettuccine, toss in the remaining olive oil and transfer to a warmed serving dish. Spoon the anchovy and spinach sauce over the fettuccine, toss lightly and serve immediately.

baked tuna & ricotta rigatoni

⏱ **cook: 10 mins**   🕐 **prep: 45 mins**   **serves 4**

Ribbed tubes of pasta are filled with tuna and ricotta cheese and then baked in a delicious creamy sauce.

NUTRITIONAL INFORMATION	
Calories	.949
Protein	.51g
Carbohydrate	.85g
Sugars	.5g
Fat	.48g
Saturates	.26g

INGREDIENTS

butter, for greasing

1 lb/450 g dried rigatoni

7 oz/200 g canned flaked tuna, drained

1 cup ricotta cheese

½ cup heavy cream

2 cups freshly grated Parmesan cheese

salt and pepper

4 oz/115 g sun-dried tomatoes, drained
and sliced

variation

For a vegetarian alternative of this recipe, simply substitute a mixture of pitted and chopped black olives and chopped walnuts for the tuna. Follow exactly the same cooking method.

1 Preheat the oven to 400°F/200°C. Lightly grease a large ovenproof dish with butter. Bring a large, heavy-bottom pan of lightly salted water to a boil. Add the rigatoni, return to a boil and cook for 8–10 minutes, or until just tender but still firm to the bite. Drain the pasta and leave until cool enough to handle.

2 Meanwhile, mix the tuna and ricotta cheese together in a bowl to form a soft paste. Spoon the mixture into a pastry bag and use to fill the rigatoni. Arrange the filled pasta tubes side by side in the prepared dish.

3 To make the sauce, mix the cream and Parmesan cheese together in a

bowl and season to taste with salt and pepper. Spoon the sauce over the rigatoni and top with the sun-dried tomatoes, arranged in a criss-cross pattern. Bake in the preheated oven for 20 minutes. Serve hot straight from the dish.

meat & poultry

Both beef and chicken are indisputably the classic partners for pasta—think of Spaghetti & Meatballs (see page 65), Lasagna al Forno (see page 70), or Creamy Chicken Ravioli (see page 101). That said, you may be pleasantly surprised by some rather different recipes, such as Pepperoni Pasta (see page 78), Chile Pork with Tagliatelle (see page 81), and Bucatini with Lamb & Yellow Pepper Sauce (see page 88). One of the great joys of pasta dishes is that there is always at least one that is exactly right, whatever the occasion, season, level of culinary skill, time available, and extent of the budget. There are speedy midweek suppers to feed a hungry family, robust baked dishes to take the chill off winter evenings, delicately flavored filled pasta that is ideal for entertaining, and hot and spicy mixtures to set the taste buds tingling.

Meat and poultry are combined with herbs, wine, olives, mushrooms, cheese, bell peppers, and, of course, tomatoes to make fabulous sauces and fillings for every kind of pasta, from curly corkscrew fusilli to long strings of linguine and from bulging cannelloni tubes to the little buttons of tortellini that are said to resemble Venus's navel. Whether you plan to make your own dough for preparing ravioli or you have not planned at all and must ransack the refrigerator and pantry for whatever is to hand, there is a perfect pasta dish to fit the bill.

classic tagliatelle bolognese

serves 4   **prep: 15 mins**   **cook: 50–55 mins**

Bologna is a close culinary rival to Rome and boasts some of the best restaurants in Italy. This signature dish is classically made with tagliatelle, rather than spaghetti.

INGREDIENTS

4 tbsp olive oil, plus extra for drizzling

3 oz/85 g pancetta or rindless lean bacon, diced

1 onion, chopped

1 garlic clove, finely chopped

1 carrot, chopped

1 celery stalk, chopped

1 cup fresh ground beef

4 oz/115 g chicken livers, chopped

2 tbsp strained tomatoes

½ cup dry white wine

1 cup Beef Stock (see page 12) or water

1 tbsp chopped fresh oregano or marjoram

1 bay leaf

salt and pepper

1 lb/450 g dried tagliatelle

freshly grated Parmesan cheese, to serve

NUTRITIONAL INFORMATION

Calories	.700
Protein	.35g
Carbohydrate	.89g
Sugars	.8g
Fat	.24g
Saturates	.5g

variation

For a chunky sauce, replace the ground beef with the same amount of finely chopped fresh braising steak.

cook's tip

Cheap ground beef is a false economy, as it is very fatty. Look for lean ground beef or, better still, buy good-quality steak and grind it yourself.

1 Heat the olive oil in a large, heavy-bottom pan. Add the diced pancetta and cook over medium heat, stirring occasionally, for 3–5 minutes, or until turning brown. Add the onion, garlic, carrot, and celery and cook, stirring occasionally, for an additional 5 minutes.

2 Add the beef and cook over high heat, breaking up the meat with a wooden spoon, for 5 minutes, or until browned. Stir in the chicken livers and cook, stirring occasionally, for an additional 2–3 minutes. Add the strained tomatoes, wine, Beef Stock, oregano, and bay leaf, and season to taste with salt and

pepper. Bring to a boil, reduce the heat, cover, and let simmer for 30–35 minutes.

3 Meanwhile, bring a large, heavy-bottom pan of lightly salted water to a boil. Add the pasta, return to a boil, and cook for 8–10 minutes, or until tender but still firm to the bite. Drain,

transfer to a warmed serving dish, drizzle with a little olive oil, and toss well. Remove and discard the bay leaf from the sauce, then pour it onto the pasta, toss again, and serve with grated Parmesan cheese.

spaghetti & meatballs

⏱ cook: 45 mins

⏱ prep: 20 mins, plus
30 mins chilling

serves 6

NUTRITIONAL INFORMATION	
Calories 280	
Protein 18g	
Carbohydrate 40g	
Sugars 3g	
Fat 7g	
Saturates 1g	

variation

For a spicier version, substitute a pinch of crushed, dried red chile for the cayenne and stir ½ teaspoon crushed chile into the sauce with the sugar.

A very popular dish with both children and adults, in which delicious, bite-size meatballs are simmered in a rich tomato sauce and served on a bed of freshly cooked spaghetti.

INGREDIENTS

1 oz/25 g white bread, crusts removed
and torn into pieces

2 tbsp milk

2 cups fresh ground beef

4 tbsp chopped fresh
flatleaf parsley

1 egg

pinch of cayenne pepper

salt and pepper

2 tbsp olive oil

⅔ cup strained tomatoes

7 oz/200 g canned chopped tomatoes

1¾ cups Vegetable Stock
(see page 12)

pinch of sugar

1 lb/450 g dried spaghetti

cook's tip

When forming the meat mixture into balls, dampen your hands slightly with a little cold water to help prevent the mixture sticking.

1 Place the bread in a small bowl, add the milk and let soak. Meanwhile, place the beef in a large bowl and add half the parsley, the egg, and the cayenne pepper. Season to taste with salt and pepper. Squeeze the excess moisture out of the bread and crumble it over the meat mixture. Mix well until smooth.

2 Form small pieces of the mixture into balls between the palms of your hands and place on a baking sheet or board. Let chill in the refrigerator for 30 minutes.

3 Heat the olive oil in a heavy-bottom skillet. Add the meatballs in batches, and cook, stirring and turning frequently, until browned on all sides. Return earlier batches to the skillet, add the strained tomatoes, chopped tomatoes and their can juices, Vegetable Stock, and sugar, then season to taste with salt and pepper. Bring to a boil, reduce the heat, cover, and let simmer for 25–30 minutes, or until the sauce is thickened and the meatballs are tender and cooked through.

4 Meanwhile, bring a large, heavy-bottom pan of lightly salted water to a boil. Add the pasta, return to a boil, and cook for 8–10 minutes, or until tender but still firm to the bite. Drain and transfer to a warmed serving dish. Pour the sauce over the pasta and toss lightly. Sprinkle with the remaining parsley and serve immediately.

pasta soufflé

serves 4　　　　　prep: 20 mins ⏲　　　　　cook: 1 hr 15 mins ⏲

A variation on the classic pasta bolognese, this is an economical dish that is perfect for family meals and informal entertaining.

INGREDIENTS

2 tbsp olive oil	salt and pepper
1 large onion, chopped	6 oz/175 g dried elbow macaroni
1 cup fresh ground beef	butter, for greasing
1 garlic clove, finely chopped	3 eggs, separated
14 oz/400 g canned chopped tomatoes	⅜ cup freshly grated Parmesan cheese,
1 tbsp tomato paste	plus extra for sprinkling

NUTRITIONAL INFORMATION

Calories 427

Protein 28g

Carbohydrate 42g

Sugars 8g

Fat 18g

Saturates 6g

variation

Substitute the dried elbow macaroni with other dried small pasta shapes, such as penne, conchiglie, or rigatoni.

cook's tip

Parmesan cheese is an Italian hard cheese made from skim milk. If possible, try to buy fresh Parmesan cheese in a block and grate it yourself as its flavor is far superior to that of the dried cheese.

1 Preheat the oven to 375°F/190°C. Heat the olive oil in a large, heavy-bottom skillet. Add the onion and cook over low heat, stirring occasionally, for 5 minutes, or until softened. Add the beef and cook, breaking up the meat with a wooden spoon, until browned. Stir in the garlic, tomatoes and their can juices, and tomato

paste, then season to taste with salt and pepper. Bring to a boil, reduce the heat, and let simmer for 20 minutes, then remove the skillet from the heat and let cool slightly.

2 Meanwhile, bring a large, heavy-bottom pan of lightly salted water to a boil. Add the pasta, return to a boil, and cook for

8–10 minutes, or until tender but still firm to the bite. Drain and set aside.

3 Lightly grease a 5-cup soufflé dish with butter. Beat the egg yolks and add them to the meat sauce, then stir in the pasta. Whisk the egg whites until stiff peaks form, then fold into the sauce. Spoon the mixture into the

dish, sprinkle with the grated Parmesan cheese, and bake in the preheated oven for 45 minutes, or until well risen and golden brown. Sprinkle with extra grated Parmesan cheese and serve immediately.

beef & spaghetti surprise

serves 4 **prep: 30 mins** **cook: 1 hr 30 mins**

This delicious Sicilian recipe originated as a handy way of using up leftover cooked pasta.

INGREDIENTS

⅔ cup olive oil, plus extra
for brushing

2 eggplants

12 oz/350 g fresh ground beef

1 onion, chopped

2 garlic cloves, crushed

2 tbsp tomato paste

14 oz/400 g canned chopped tomatoes

1 tsp Worcestershire sauce

1 tsp chopped fresh marjoram or
oregano, or ½ tsp dried marjoram
or oregano

salt and pepper

18 pitted black olives, sliced

1 green, red or yellow bell pepper,
cored, seeded, and chopped

6 oz/175 g dried spaghetti

1 cup freshly grated Parmesan cheese

fresh oregano or parsley sprigs,
to garnish

NUTRITIONAL INFORMATION

Calories 797

Protein 31g

Carbohydrate 35g

Sugars 7g

Fat 60g

Saturates 16g

variation

You can use ground lamb instead of
the ground beef and tagliatelle instead
of the spaghetti, if you prefer.

cook's tip

When buying eggplants, look
for ones that have a glossy skin
and feel heavy. Avoid those
with dull and bruised skins.

1 Preheat the oven to
400°F/200°C. Brush an
8-inch/20-cm springform
round cake pan with oil, line
the base with parchment
paper and brush with olive oil.

2 Slice the eggplants.
Heat a little olive oil
in a pan and cook the
eggplant, in batches, for
3–4 minutes, or until browned

on both sides. Add more oil,
as necessary. Drain on paper
towels. Place the ground beef,
onion, and garlic in a separate
pan and cook over medium
heat, stirring occasionally,
until browned. Add the
tomato paste, tomatoes,
Worcestershire sauce,
marjoram, and add salt and
pepper to taste. Let simmer,
stirring occasionally, for

10 minutes. Add the olives
and bell pepper, and cook for
an additional 10 minutes.

3 Bring a large pan of
salted water to a boil.
Add the pasta, return to a boil
and cook for 8–10 minutes, or
until tender but still firm to
the bite. Drain and transfer
the pasta to a bowl. Add the
meat mixture and cheese, and

toss with 2 forks. Arrange the
eggplant slices over the base
and up the sides of the
springform pan. Add the pasta,
pressing down firmly, then
cover with the rest of the
eggplant. Bake in the oven
for 40 minutes. Let stand for
5 minutes, then invert onto a
plate. Discard the parchment
paper. Garnish with herbs
and serve.

lasagna al forno

serves 4   **prep: 15 mins** ⟳   **cook: 1 hr 15 mins** ⏲

Layers of pasta, meat sauce, and lasagna, all covered with a rich cheese sauce, makes a tasty and substantial family supper.

INGREDIENTS

2 tbsp olive oil

2 oz/55 g pancetta or rindless lean bacon, chopped

1 onion, chopped

1 garlic clove, finely chopped

1 cup fresh ground beef

2 celery stalks, chopped

2 carrots, chopped

salt and pepper

pinch of sugar

½ tsp dried oregano

14 oz/400 g canned chopped tomatoes

8 oz/225 g dried no-precook lasagna

1 cup freshly grated Parmesan cheese, plus extra for sprinkling

CHEESE SAUCE

2 tsp Dijon mustard

2½ oz/70 g Cheddar cheese, grated

2½ oz/70 g Gruyère cheese, grated

1¼ cups hot Béchamel Sauce (see page 12)

variation

Substitute the Gruyère cheese with another good melting cheese, such as Emmental, if you prefer.

cook's tip

You can use either plain or egg lasagna sheets in this dish. They are available in three colors: plain lasagna is yellow, spinach lasagna or lasagna verde is green, while whole-wheat lasagna is brown.

1 Preheat the oven to 375°F/190°C. Heat the olive oil in a large, heavy-bottom pan. Add the pancetta and cook over medium heat, stirring occasionally, for 3 minutes, or until the fat starts to run. Add the onion and garlic and cook, stirring occasionally, for 5 minutes, or until softened.

2 Add the beef and cook, breaking it up with a wooden spoon, until browned all over. Stir in the celery and carrot and cook for 5 minutes. Season to taste with salt and pepper. Add the sugar, oregano, and tomatoes and their can juices. Bring to a boil, reduce the heat, and let simmer for 30 minutes.

3 Meanwhile, to make the cheese sauce, stir the mustard and both cheeses into the hot Béchamel Sauce.

4 In a large, rectangular ovenproof dish, make alternate layers of meat sauce, lasagna, and Parmesan cheese. Pour the cheese sauce over the layers, covering them

completely, and sprinkle with Parmesan cheese. Bake in the preheated oven for 30 minutes, or until golden brown and bubbling. Serve immediately.

mixed meat lasagna

serves 6   **prep: 20 mins**   **cook: 1 hr 35 mins**

This is a wonderful dish for an informal supper party. Serve with a crisp green salad, some crusty Italian bread, and, perhaps, a bottle or two of red wine.

INGREDIENTS

1 onion, chopped	1 clove
1 carrot, chopped	salt and pepper
1 celery stalk, chopped	⅔ cup milk
3 oz/85 g pancetta or rindless	4 tbsp butter, diced, plus extra
lean bacon, chopped	for greasing
¾ cup fresh ground beef	14 oz/400 g dried no-precook
¾ cup fresh ground pork	lasagna verde
3 tbsp olive oil	2½ cups Béchamel Sauce
generous ⅓ cup red wine	(see page 12)
⅔ cup Beef Stock (see page 12)	1¼ cups freshly grated
1 tbsp tomato paste	Parmesan cheese
1 bay leaf	5 oz/140 g mozzarella cheese, diced

NUTRITIONAL INFORMATION

Calories	.810
Protein	.43g
Carbohydrate	.65g
Sugars	.11g
Fat	.41g
Saturates	.21g

variation

For a lighter dish, substitute fresh ground chicken for the ground beef and pork and Chicken Stock for the Beef Stock (see page 12).

cook's tip

Bay leaves are available in both fresh and dried forms. Always use sparingly as their strong flavor can be overwhelming. They are best used in robust, well-flavored dishes.

1 Mix the chopped onion, carrot, celery, pancetta, beef, and pork together in a large bowl. Heat the olive oil in a large, heavy-bottom skillet, add the meat mixture and cook over medium heat, breaking up the meat with a wooden spoon, until it is browned all over. Pour in the red wine, then bring to a boil and cook until reduced. Pour

in ½ cup of the Beef Stock, bring to a boil and cook until reduced.

2 Mix the tomato paste and remaining Beef Stock together in a small bowl, then add to the skillet with the bay leaf and clove. Season to taste with salt and pepper and pour in the milk. Cover and let simmer for 1 hour.

3 Preheat the oven to 400°F/200°C. Remove and discard the bay leaf and the clove from the meat sauce. Lightly grease a large, ovenproof dish with butter. Make alternate layers of lasagna, meat sauce, Béchamel Sauce, and Parmesan and mozzarella cheese in the dish, ending with Béchamel Sauce sprinkled with cheese.

4 Dot the top of the lasagna with butter and bake in the preheated oven for 25 minutes, or until golden brown. Serve immediately.

lasagna verde

serves 6   **prep: 1 hr 45 mins** ⟳   **cook: 55 mins** ⟳

This baked pasta dish is extremely easy to make and is the ideal choice for any occasion. It is particularly good served with plenty of salad.

INGREDIENTS

Ragù Sauce (see page 62)

8 oz/225 g lasagna verde

butter, for greasing

Béchamel Sauce (see page 12)

½ cup freshly grated Parmesan cheese

salt and pepper

green salad, tomato salad, or

black olives, to serve

NUTRITIONAL INFORMATION	
Calories 619	
Protein 29g	
Carbohydrate 21g	
Sugars 7g	
Fat 45g	
Saturates 19g	

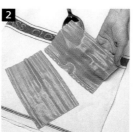

variation

If lasagna verde pasta sheets are unavailable, then use plain lasagna pasta sheets instead.

1 Preheat the oven to 375°F/190°C. Begin by making the Ragù Sauce as described on page 62, steps 1 and 2, but cook for 10–12 minutes longer than the time given, in an uncovered pan, to allow the excess liquid to evaporate. To layer the sauce with lasagne, it needs to be reduced to the consistency of a thick paste.

2 Have ready a large pan of boiling, salted water. Drop the pasta sheets into the boiling water a few at a time, and return the water to a boil before adding further pasta sheets. If you are using fresh pasta, cook the sheets for a total of 8 minutes. If you are using dried or partly precooked pasta, cook it according to the package instructions.

Remove the pasta sheets with a slotted spoon. Spread them in a single layer on damp dish towels.

3 Grease a rectangular ovenproof dish, about 10–11 inches/25–28 cm long. To assemble the dish, spoon a little of the meat sauce into the prepared dish, cover with a layer of pasta, then spoon

over a little Béchamel Sauce and sprinkle with some of the cheese. Continue making layers in this way, covering the final layer of pasta with the remaining Béchamel Sauce. Sprinkle on the remaining cheese and bake for 40 minutes, or until the sauce is golden and bubbling. Serve with a green salad, a tomato salad, or a bowl of black olives.

pasta carbonara

cook: 20 mins **prep: 15 mins** **serves 4**

Lightly cooked eggs and pancetta are combined with cheese to make this rich, classic sauce.

NUTRITIONAL INFORMATION	
Calories	.547
Protein	.21g
Carbohydrate	.49g
Sugars	.1g
Fat	.31g
Saturates	.14g

INGREDIENTS

1 tbsp olive oil

3 tbsp butter

3½ oz/100 g pancetta or unsmoked bacon, diced

3 eggs, beaten

2 tbsp milk

1 tbsp fresh thyme, stalks removed

salt and pepper

1 lb 8 oz/675 g fresh or 12 oz/350 g dried conchigoni rigati

½ cup freshly grated Parmesan cheese

variation

For an extra rich Carbonara sauce, stir in 4 tablespoons of heavy cream with the eggs and milk in Step 3. Follow exactly the same cooking method.

1 Heat the oil and butter together in a skillet until the mixture is just beginning to froth. Add the pancetta or bacon to the pan and cook for 5 minutes or until browned all over.

2 Mix the eggs and milk together in a bowl. Stir in the thyme and season to taste with salt and pepper.

3 Bring a large, heavy-bottom pan of lightly salted water to a boil. Add the pasta, return to a boil and cook for 8–10 minutes, or until tender but still firm to the bite. Drain thoroughly. Add the pasta to the skillet with the eggs and cook over high heat for 30 seconds, or until the eggs just begin to cook and set. Do not overcook the eggs or they will become rubbery. Add half of the grated Parmesan cheese, stirring to mix well.

4 Transfer the pasta to a serving plate. Sprinkle the rest of the grated Parmesan cheese over the top and serve immediately.

sicilian linguine

⏲ **cook: 1 hr 15 mins**   ⏱ **prep: 20 mins**   **serves 4**

This delicious classic dish of eggplants, tomatoes, meat, and olives is perfect for both a family midweek supper or a special occasion main course. Serve with a fresh green salad.

variation

Other types of long pasta also work well in this dish, such as spaghetti. Replace the red bell pepper with a yellow bell pepper, if you like.

INGREDIENTS

½ cup olive oil

2 eggplants, sliced

1½ cups fresh ground beef

1 onion, chopped

2 garlic cloves, finely chopped

2 tbsp tomato paste

14 oz/400 g canned chopped tomatoes

1 tsp Worcestershire sauce

1 tbsp chopped fresh flatleaf parsley

salt and pepper

⅓ cup pitted black olives, sliced

1 red bell pepper, seeded and chopped

6 oz/175 g dried linguine

1 cup freshly grated Parmesan cheese

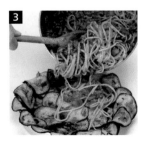

cook's tip

After cooking the eggplants, let them drain on paper towels for a few minutes because they tend to absorb quite a lot of the oil during the cooking and may make the finished dish quite oily.

1 Preheat the oven to 400°F/200°C. Brush an 8-inch/20-cm loose-bottom round cake pan with oil and line the bottom with parchment paper. Heat half the oil in a skillet. Add the eggplants in batches, and cook until lightly browned on both sides. Add more oil, as required. Drain the eggplants on paper towels, then arrange in overlapping slices to cover the bottom and sides of the cake pan, reserving a few slices.

2 Heat the remaining olive oil in a large pan and add the beef, onion, and garlic. Cook over medium heat, breaking up the meat with a wooden spoon, until browned all over. Add the tomato paste, tomatoes and their can juices, Worcestershire sauce, and parsley. Season to taste with salt and pepper and let simmer for 10 minutes. Add the olives and bell pepper and cook for 10 minutes.

3 Meanwhile, bring a pan of lightly salted water to a boil. Add the pasta, return to a boil, and cook for 8–10 minutes, or until tender but still firm to the bite. Drain and transfer to a bowl. Add the meat sauce and cheese and toss, then spoon into the cake pan, press down and cover with the remaining eggplant slices. Bake for 40 minutes. Let stand for 5 minutes, then loosen round the edges and invert onto a plate. Remove and discard the parchment paper and serve.

pepperoni pasta

serves 4   **prep: 10 mins** ⟲   **cook: 20 mins** ⏱

*Quick and easy, colorful and scrumptious—what more could a
hungry family want for a midweek supper?*

INGREDIENTS

3 tbsp olive oil

1 onion, chopped

1 red bell pepper, seeded and diced

1 orange bell pepper, seeded and diced

1 lb 12 oz/800 g canned
chopped tomatoes

1 tbsp sun-dried tomato paste

1 tsp paprika

8 oz/225 g pepperoni sausage, sliced

2 tbsp chopped fresh flatleaf parsley,

plus extra to garnish

salt and pepper

1 lb/450 g dried garganelli

mixed salad greens, to serve

NUTRITIONAL INFORMATION

Calories 707

Protein 27g

Carbohydrate 98g

Sugars 16g

Fat 26g

Saturates 7g

---

variation

If you cannot find garganelli pasta,
then use penne or another pasta
shape, such as fusilli bucati or farfalle.

cook's tip

Pepperoni is a hotly spiced
Italian sausage made from pork
and beef and is flavored with
fennel. You could substitute
other spicy sausages, such as
kabanos or chorizo, if you like.

1 Heat 2 tablespoons of
the olive oil in a large
heavy-bottom skillet. Add the
onion and cook over low heat,
stirring occasionally, for
5 minutes, or until softened.
Add the red and orange bell
peppers, tomatoes and their
can juices, sun-dried tomato
paste, and paprika and bring
to a boil.

2 Add the pepperoni and
parsley and season to
taste with salt and pepper.
Stir well, bring to a boil, then
reduce the heat and let simmer
for 10–15 minutes.

3 Meanwhile, bring a
large heavy-bottom pan
of lightly salted water to a boil.
Add the pasta, return to a boil,

and cook for 8–10 minutes, or
until tender but still firm to
the bite. Drain well and
transfer to a warmed serving
dish. Add the remaining olive
oil and toss. Add the sauce
and toss again. Sprinkle with
parsley and serve immediately
with mixed salad greens.

chile pork with tagliatelle

⏱ **cook: 10 mins**   ⏱ **prep: 10 mins**   **serves 4**

variation

Substitute the pork fillet with the same amount of skinless, boneless chicken breast, cut into thin strips. Make sure it is thoroughly cooked before serving.

East meets West in this spicy dish. However, if you want a more authentically Asian-style meal, you could serve the sauce with egg or cellophane noodles.

INGREDIENTS

1 lb/450 g dried tagliatelle

3 tbsp peanut oil

12 oz/350 g pork fillet, cut into thin strips

1 garlic clove, finely chopped

1 bunch of scallions, sliced

1-inch/2.5-cm piece fresh gingerroot, grated

2 fresh Thai chiles, seeded and finely chopped

1 red bell pepper, seeded and cut into thin sticks

1 yellow bell pepper, seeded and cut into thin sticks

3 zucchini, cut into thin sticks

2 tbsp finely chopped peanuts

1 tsp ground cinnamon

1 tbsp oyster sauce

2 oz/55 g creamed coconut, grated

salt and pepper

2 tbsp chopped fresh cilantro, to garnish

cook's tip

Thai chiles, popular in Thai cuisine, are small and pointed and may be red, white, orange, or green. They are invariably very hot. If you prefer a milder flavor use serrano or Anaheim chiles.

1 Bring a large heavy-bottom pan of lightly salted water to a boil. Add the pasta, return to a boil, and cook for 8–10 minutes, or until tender but still firm to the bite.

2 Meanwhile, heat the peanut oil in a preheated wok or large heavy-bottom skillet. Add the pork and stir-fry for 5 minutes. Add the garlic, scallions, ginger, and Thai chiles, and stir-fry for 2 minutes.

3 Add the red and yellow bell peppers and the zucchini and stir-fry for 1 minute. Add the peanuts, cinnamon, oyster sauce, and creamed coconut, and stir-fry for an additional 1 minute. Season to taste with salt and pepper. Drain the pasta and transfer to a serving dish. Top with the chile pork, sprinkle with the chopped cilantro, and serve.

pork & pasta bake

serves 4   **prep: 20 mins** ⏲   **cook: 1 hr 15 mins** ⏱

This warm and filling dish is virtually a meal in itself—perfect for a cold winter's evening. Serve it with mixed green and red salad greens, if you like.

INGREDIENTS

2 tbsp olive oil

1 onion, chopped

1 garlic clove, finely chopped

2 carrots, diced

2 oz/55 g pancetta or rindless lean bacon, chopped

4 oz/115 g mushrooms, chopped

2 cups fresh ground pork

½ cup dry white wine

4 tbsp strained tomatoes

7 oz/200 g canned chopped tomatoes

2 tsp chopped fresh sage or ½ tsp dried sage

salt and pepper

8 oz/225 g dried elicoidali or rigatoni

5 oz/140 g mozzarella cheese, diced

4 tbsp freshly grated Parmesan cheese

1¼ cups hot Béchamel Sauce (see page 12)

NUTRITIONAL INFORMATION

Calories 796

Protein 52g

Carbohydrate 59g

Sugars 13g

Fat 39g

Saturates 18g

variation

Substitute the strained tomatoes with the same amount of tomato paste and the canned tomatoes with fresh plum tomatoes, peeled and finely chopped.

cook's tip

When cooking with olive oil, try not to use extra virgin olive oil as the flavor will be lost during cooking. Olive oil is best stored in a cool place, out of direct sunlight. Do not store in the refrigerator.

1 Preheat the oven to 400°F/200°C. Heat the olive oil in a large heavy-bottom skillet. Add the onion, garlic, and carrots, and cook over low heat, stirring occasionally, for 5 minutes, or until the onion has softened. Add the pancetta and cook for 5 minutes. Add the chopped mushrooms and cook, stirring occasionally, for an additional

2 minutes. Add the ground pork and cook, breaking it up with a wooden spoon, until the meat is browned all over. Stir in the wine, strained tomatoes, chopped tomatoes and their can juices, and the chopped sage. Season to taste with salt and pepper, bring to a boil, then cover and let simmer over low heat for 25–30 minutes.

2 Meanwhile, bring a large heavy-bottom pan of lightly salted water to a boil. Add the pasta, return to a boil, and cook for 8–10 minutes, or until tender but still firm to the bite.

3 Spoon the pork mixture into a large ovenproof dish. Stir the mozzarella and half the Parmesan cheese into

the Béchamel Sauce. Drain the pasta and stir the sauce into it, then spoon it over the pork mixture. Sprinkle with the remaining Parmesan cheese and bake in the oven for 25–30 minutes, or until golden brown. Serve immediately.

pasta & pork in cream sauce

serves 4   **prep: 45 mins** ⟲   **cook: 35 mins** ⟳

This unusual and attractive dish is extremely delicious. Make the Red Wine Sauce in advance to reduce the preparation time.

INGREDIENTS

1 lb/450 g pork fillet,
thinly sliced

4 tbsp olive oil

8 oz/225 g white mushrooms, sliced

1 tbsp lemon juice

pinch of saffron threads

12 oz/350 g dried orecchioni

4 tbsp heavy cream

12 quail eggs (see Cook's Tip)

salt

RED WINE SAUCE

1 tbsp olive oil

1 onion, chopped

1 tbsp tomato paste

¾ cup red wine

1 tsp oregano, finely chopped

NUTRITIONAL INFORMATION

Calories 735

Protein 31g

Carbohydrate 37g

Sugars 4g

Fat 52g

Saturates 19g

variation

Substitute the orecchioni with other small pasta shapes and replace the white mushrooms with cremini mushrooms, if you prefer.

cook's tip

In this recipe, the quail eggs are soft-cooked. As they are extremely difficult to shell when warm, it is important that they are thoroughly cooled first. Otherwise, they will break up.

1 To make the Red Wine Sauce heat the oil in a small heavy-bottom pan, add the chopped onion, and cook until transparent. Stir in the tomato paste, red wine, and oregano. Heat gently to reduce and set aside.

2 Pound the slices of pork between 2 sheets of plastic wrap until wafer thin, then cut into strips. Heat the oil in a skillet, add the pork, and stir-fry for 5 minutes. Add the mushrooms to the skillet and stir-fry for an additional 2 minutes. Strain and pour over the Red Wine Sauce. Reduce the heat and let simmer for 20 minutes.

3 Meanwhile, bring a large heavy-bottom pan of lightly salted water to a boil. Add the lemon juice, saffron, and orecchioni, return to a boil and cook for 8–10 minutes, or until tender but still firm to the bite. Drain the pasta thoroughly, return to the pan, and keep warm.

4 Stir the cream into the pan with the pork and heat for a few minutes.

5 Boil the quail eggs for 3 minutes, cool them in cold water and remove the shells.Transfer the pasta to a large, warmed serving plate, top with the pork and the sauce, and garnish with the eggs. Serve immediately.

pasticcio

⏱ **cook: 1 hr 40 mins**   🕐 **prep: 15 mins**   **serves 4**

NUTRITIONAL INFORMATION	
Calories	.512
Protein	.38g
Carbohydrate	.40g
Sugars	.8g
Fat	.24g
Saturates	.10g

Not every pasta recipe has its origins in Italy. This is a traditional Greek bake made with lamb. It is delicious served hot or cold.

INGREDIENTS

1 tbsp olive oil

1 onion, chopped

2 garlic cloves, finely chopped

2 cups fresh ground lamb

2 tbsp tomato paste

2 tbsp all-purpose flour

1¼ cups Chicken Stock
(see page 12)

salt and pepper

1 tsp ground cinnamon

4 oz/115 g dried short-cut macaroni

2 beefsteak tomatoes, sliced

1¼ cups strained plain yogurt

2 eggs, lightly beaten

variation

Pasticcio is also delicious made with fresh ground turkey or chicken. Replace the strained plain yogurt with plain yogurt, if you like.

cook's tip

If the meat sauce is too runny, then add an extra tablespoon of flour to the sauce and cook, stirring constantly, until the sauce has thickened slightly.

1 Preheat the oven to 375°F/190°C. Heat the olive oil in a large heavy-bottom skillet. Add the onion and garlic and cook over low heat, stirring occasionally, for 5 minutes, or until softened. Add the lamb and cook, breaking it up with a wooden spoon, until browned all over. Add the tomato paste and sprinkle in the flour. Cook,

stirring, for 1 minute, then stir in the Chicken Stock. Season to taste with salt and pepper and stir in the cinnamon. Bring to a boil, reduce the heat, cover, and cook for 25 minutes.

2 Meanwhile, bring a large heavy-bottom pan of lightly salted water to a boil. Add the pasta, return to a boil,

and cook for 8–10 minutes, or until tender but still firm to the bite.

3 Spoon the lamb mixture into a large ovenproof dish and arrange the tomato slices on top. Drain the pasta and transfer to a bowl. Add the yogurt and eggs and mix well. Spoon the pasta mixture on top of the

lamb and bake in the preheated oven for 1 hour. Serve immediately.

bucatini with lamb & yellow pepper sauce

serves 4   **prep: 10 mins**   **cook: 1 hr**

This regional specialty is traditionally served with square-shaped macaroni, but this is not widely available. That said, you may find it in an Italian delicatessen. This recipe uses bucatini instead.

INGREDIENTS

4 tbsp olive oil

10 oz/280 g boneless lamb, cubed

1 garlic clove, finely chopped

1 bay leaf

1 cup dry white wine

salt and pepper

2 large yellow bell peppers, seeded
and diced

4 tomatoes, peeled and chopped

9 oz/250 g dried bucatini

NUTRITIONAL INFORMATION	
Calories	704
Protein	. . . . .31g
Carbohydrate	. . . . .98g
Sugars	. . . . .10g
Fat	. . . . .20g
Saturates	. . . . .5g

cook's tip

cook's tip

Bucatini is a long, thin, hollow pasta. If you are unable to find bucatini, then substitute spaghetti or another similar type of long pasta instead.

1 Heat half the olive oil in a large heavy-bottom skillet. Add the lamb and cook over medium heat, stirring frequently, until browned on all sides. Add the garlic and cook for an additional 1 minute. Add the bay leaf, pour in the wine, and season to taste with salt and pepper. Bring to a boil and cook for 5 minutes, or until reduced.

2 Stir in the remaining oil, bell peppers, and tomatoes. Reduce the heat, cover, and let simmer, stirring occasionally, for 45 minutes.

3 Meanwhile, bring a large heavy-bottom pan of lightly salted water to a boil. Add the pasta, return to a boil, and cook for 8–10 minutes, or until tender but still firm to the bite. Drain and transfer to a warmed serving dish. Remove and discard the bay leaf from the lamb sauce and spoon the sauce onto the pasta. Toss well and serve immediately.

spaghetti with parsley chicken

cook: 15 mins　　　　**prep: 15 mins**　　　　**serves 4**

Lemon, ginger, and fresh flatleaf parsley give an extra lift to the chicken and pasta in this lovely summery dish. Use fresh spaghetti instead of the dried, if you prefer.

NUTRITIONAL INFORMATION

Calories	.430
Protein	.21g
Carbohydrate	.52g
Sugars	.7g
Fat	.17g
Saturates	.8g

INGREDIENTS

1 tbsp olive oil

thinly pared rind of 1 lemon, cut into julienne strips

1 tsp finely chopped fresh gingerroot

1 tsp sugar

salt

1 cup Chicken Stock (see page 12)

9 oz/250 g dried spaghetti

4 tbsp butter

8 oz/225 g skinless, boneless chicken breasts, diced

1 red onion, finely chopped

leaves from 2 bunches of flatleaf parsley

cook's tip

Use an unwaxed lemon, if possible, and wash before paring the rind. If only waxed lemons are available—or you are not sure—scrub with a vegetable brush.

1 Heat the olive oil in a heavy-bottom pan. Add the lemon rind and cook over low heat, stirring frequently, for 5 minutes. Stir in the ginger and sugar, season to taste with salt, and cook, stirring constantly, for an additional 2 minutes. Pour in the Chicken Stock, bring to a boil, then cook for 5 minutes, or until the liquid has reduced by half.

2 Meanwhile, bring a large heavy-bottom pan of lightly salted water to a boil. Add the pasta, return to a boil, and cook for 8–10 minutes, or until tender but still firm to the bite.

3 Meanwhile, melt half the butter in a skillet. Add the chicken and onion and cook, stirring frequently, for 5 minutes, or until the chicken is light brown all over. Stir in the lemon and ginger mixture and cook for 1 minute. Stir in the parsley leaves and cook, stirring constantly, for an additional 3 minutes.

4 Drain the pasta and transfer to a warmed serving dish, then add the remaining butter and toss well. Add the chicken sauce, toss again, and serve.

pasta & lamb loaf

serves 4 **prep: 10 mins, plus** ⏲ **25 mins standing** **cook: 35 mins** ⏲

Any dried pasta shape can be used for this delicious recipe. It has been adapted here for microwave cooking for convenience.

INGREDIENTS

1 tbsp butter	1 tsp dried mixed herbs
½ small eggplant, diced	2 eggs, beaten
salt and pepper	2 tbsp light cream
2 oz/55 g multicolored fusilli	
2 tsp olive oil	TO SERVE
1 cup fresh ground lamb	salad
½ small onion, chopped	pasta sauce of your choice
½ red bell pepper, chopped	
1 garlic clove, crushed	

NUTRITIONAL INFORMATION

Calories	245
Protein	. . . . .15g
Carbohydrate	. . . . .6g
Sugars	. . . . .2g
Fat	. . . . .18g
Saturates	. . . . .7g

variation

Use a shallot instead of a small onion and replace the red bell pepper with an orange one, if you prefer.

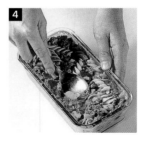

cook's tip

You can add any pasta sauce of your choice to this recipe, such as Red Sauce (see page 108) or Cheese Sauce (see page 42).

1 Place the butter in a 1 lb 2-oz/500-g loaf dish. Cook on High power for 30 seconds until melted. Brush over the base and sides of the dish. Sprinkle the eggplant with salt, place in a colander and let stand for 20 minutes. Rinse the eggplant well and pat dry with paper towels.

2 Place the pasta in a bowl, add a little salt and enough boiling water to cover by 1 inch/2.5 cm. Cover and cook on High power for 8 minutes, stirring halfway through. Let stand, covered, for a few minutes.

3 Place the oil, lamb, and onion in a bowl. Cover and cook on High power for

2 minutes. Break up any lumps of meat using a fork. Add the bell pepper, garlic, herbs, and eggplant. Cover and cook on High power for 5 minutes, stirring halfway through.

4 Drain the pasta and add to the lamb with the eggs and cream. Season well with salt and pepper.

Transfer to the loaf dish and pat down using the back of a spoon. Cook on Medium power for 10 minutes, or until firm to the touch. Let stand for 5 minutes before turning out. Serve in slices with a salad and a pasta sauce.

cannelloni with ham & ricotta

serves 4   **prep: 10 mins** ⟲   **cook: 1 hr 5 mins** ⟳

More delicately flavored than the usual beef-filled cannelloni,
this is still a substantial dish for a family supper.

INGREDIENTS

2 tbsp olive oil	12 oz/350 g dried cannelloni tubes
2 onions, chopped	butter, for greasing
2 garlic cloves, finely chopped	generous 1 cup ricotta cheese
1 tbsp shredded fresh basil	4 oz/115 g cooked ham, diced
1 lb 12 oz/800 g canned	1 egg
chopped tomatoes	½ cup freshly grated
1 tbsp tomato paste	romano cheese
salt and pepper	

NUTRITIONAL INFORMATION

Calories 616

Protein 29g

Carbohydrate 81g

Sugars 15g

Fat 21g

Saturates 9g

variation

Substitute the romano cheese with
the same amount of freshly grated
Parmesan cheese, if you prefer.

cook's tip

Make sure that the cooked
cannelloni tubes are dry
before filling as they may go
soggy during cooking. Pat dry
thoroughly with paper towels
before filling with the ham
and ricotta mixture.

1 Preheat the oven to
350°F/180°C. Heat
the olive oil in a large heavy-
bottom skillet. Add the onions
and garlic and cook over low
heat, stirring occasionally, for
5 minutes, or until the onion is
softened. Add the basil,
chopped tomatoes and their
can juices, and tomato paste,
and season to taste with salt
and pepper. Reduce the heat

and let simmer for 30 minutes,
or until thickened.

2 Meanwhile, bring a
large heavy-bottom pan
of lightly salted water to a boil.
Add the cannelloni tubes,
return to a boil, and cook for
8–10 minutes, or until tender
but still firm to the bite. Using
a slotted spoon, transfer the
cannelloni tubes to a large

plate and pat dry with
paper towels.

3 Grease a large, shallow
ovenproof dish with
butter. Mix the ricotta, ham,
and egg together in a bowl
and season to taste with salt
and pepper. Using a teaspoon,
fill the cannelloni tubes with
the ricotta mixture and place
in a single layer in the dish.

Pour the tomato sauce over the
cannelloni and sprinkle with
the grated pecorino cheese.
Bake in the preheated oven for
30 minutes, or until golden
brown. Serve immediately.

linguine with bacon & olives

⏱ **cook: 10 mins**   ⏲ **prep: 10 mins**   **serves 4**

NUTRITIONAL INFORMATION

Calories	.600
Protein	.27g
Carbohydrate	.90g
Sugars	.8g
Fat	.17g
Saturates	.4g

variation

If you like, use a mixture of exotic mushrooms for extra flavor and substitute prosciutto for the bacon.

This wonderfully speedy dish, made mainly from pantry ingredients, tastes fabulous, and is great for feeding unexpected guests. Serve with salad and bread for a filling supper.

INGREDIENTS

3 tbsp olive oil

2 onions, thinly sliced

2 garlic cloves, finely chopped

6 oz/175 g rindless lean bacon, diced

8 oz/225 g mushrooms, sliced

5 canned anchovy fillets, drained

6 black olives, pitted and halved

salt and pepper

1 lb/450 g dried linguine

¼ cup freshly grated Parmesan cheese

cook's tip

You can buy olives that have been pitted already in jars or cans from most supermarkets, although try not to buy ones stored in brine as they may make the dish too salty.

1 Heat the olive oil in a large skillet. Add the onions, garlic, and bacon, and cook over low heat, stirring occasionally, until the onions are softened. Stir in the mushrooms, anchovies, and olives, then season to taste with salt, if necessary, and pepper. Simmer for 5 minutes.

2 Meanwhile, bring a large heavy-bottom pan of lightly salted water to a boil. Add the pasta, return to a boil, and cook for 8–10 minutes, or until tender but still firm to the bite.

3 Drain the pasta and transfer to a warmed serving dish. Spoon the sauce on top, toss lightly, and sprinkle with the Parmesan cheese. Serve immediately.

chicken lasagna

serves 6 | **prep: 15 mins** | **cook: 1 hr 40 mins**

This lighter variation of the classic Lasagna al Forno (see page 70) is especially popular with children.

INGREDIENTS

2 tbsp olive oil	2 tbsp tomato paste
4 cups fresh ground chicken	salt and pepper
1 garlic clove, finely chopped	4 oz/115 g Cheddar cheese, grated
4 carrots, chopped	1 tsp Dijon mustard
4 leeks, sliced	2½ cups hot Béchamel Sauce
2 cups Chicken Stock	(see page 12)
(see page 12)	4 oz/115 g dried no-precook lasagna

NUTRITIONAL INFORMATION

Calories	.570
Protein	.46g
Carbohydrate	.37g
Sugars	.13g
Fat	.27g
Saturates	.13g

variation

Substitute the fresh ground chicken with the same amount of ground turkey and add 6 oz/175 g chopped chicken livers, if you like.

cook's tip

When cooking the ground chicken, keep stirring it with a wooden spoon to break up any lumps and to seal in the flavor. Make sure it is browned all over before adding the rest of the ingredients.

1 Preheat the oven to 375°F/190°C. Heat the oil in a heavy-bottom pan. Add the chicken and cook over medium heat, breaking it up with a wooden spoon, for 5 minutes, or until it is browned all over. Add the garlic, carrots, and leeks, and cook, stirring occasionally for 5 minutes.

2 Stir in the Chicken Stock and tomato paste and season to taste with salt and pepper. Bring to a boil, reduce the heat, cover, and let simmer for 30 minutes.

3 Whisk half the Cheddar cheese and the mustard into the hot Béchamel Sauce. In a large ovenproof dish, make alternate layers of the chicken mixture, lasagna, and cheese sauce, ending with a layer of cheese sauce. Sprinkle with the remaining Cheddar cheese and bake in the preheated oven for 1 hour, or until golden brown and bubbling. Serve immediately.

chicken & exotic mushroom cannelloni

serves 4   **prep: 15 mins** ⏲   **cook: 1 hr 45 mins** ⏲

Cannelloni tubes filled with a delicious mix of exotic mushrooms, chicken, and prosciutto make a wonderful dinner party main course. Serve with a crisp green salad, if you like.

INGREDIENTS

butter, for greasing

2 tbsp olive oil

2 garlic cloves, crushed

1 large onion, finely chopped

8 oz/225 g exotic mushrooms, sliced

1½ cups fresh ground chicken

4 oz/115 g prosciutto, diced

⅔ cup Marsala wine

7 oz/200 g canned chopped tomatoes

1 tbsp shredded fresh basil leaves

2 tbsp tomato paste

salt and pepper

10–12 cannelloni tubes

2½ cups Béchamel Sauce (see page 12)

¾ cup freshly grated Parmesan cheese

NUTRITIONAL INFORMATION	
Calories 830	
Protein 48g	
Carbohydrate 62g	
Sugars 17g	
Fat 36g	
Saturates 17g	

variation

If you like, replace the Marsala wine with the same amount of brandy and substitute the canned tomatoes with the same amount of fresh tomatoes.

cook's tip

You can use any combination of exotic mushrooms. For extra flavor, add ¼ cup dried porcini, soaked in hot water for 30 minutes.

1 Preheat the oven to 375°F/190°C. Lightly grease a large ovenproof dish. Heat the olive oil in a heavy-bottom skillet. Add the garlic, onion, and mushrooms, and cook over low heat, stirring frequently, for 8–10 minutes. Add the ground chicken and prosciutto and cook, stirring frequently, for 12 minutes, or until browned all over. Stir in

the Marsala, tomatoes and their can juices, basil, and tomato paste, and cook for 4 minutes. Season to taste with salt and pepper, then cover and let simmer for 30 minutes. Uncover, stir, and let simmer for 15 minutes.

2 Meanwhile, bring a large heavy-bottom pan of lightly salted water to a boil.

Add the pasta, return to a boil, and cook for 8–10 minutes, or until tender but still firm to the bite. Using a slotted spoon, transfer the cannelloni tubes to a plate and pat dry with paper towels.

3 Using a teaspoon, fill the cannelloni tubes with the chicken and mushroom mixture. Transfer

them to the dish. Pour the Béchamel Sauce over them to cover completely and sprinkle with the grated Parmesan cheese.

4 Bake in the preheated oven for 30 minutes, or until golden brown and bubbling. Serve immediately.

creamy chicken ravioli

cook: 15 mins

prep: 30 mins, plus 1 hr resting

serves 4

Although it takes some time to prepare, this dish is extremely easy, but is sure to impress.

variation

If cremini mushrooms are unavailable, use the same amount of exotic mushrooms, such as chanterelle. Alternatively, use shiitake mushrooms.

INGREDIENTS

4 oz/115 g cooked skinless, boneless chicken breast, coarsely chopped (see Cook's Tip)

generous ⅛ cup cooked spinach

2 oz/55 g prosciutto, coarsely chopped

1 shallot, coarsely chopped

6 tbsp freshly grated romano cheese

pinch of freshly grated nutmeg

2 eggs, lightly beaten

salt and pepper

1 quantity Basic Pasta Dough (see page 13)

all-purpose flour, for dusting

1¼ cups heavy cream or panna da cucina

2 garlic cloves, finely chopped

4 oz/115 g cremini mushrooms, thinly sliced

2 tbsp shredded fresh basil

fresh basil sprigs, to garnish

cook's tip

To cook the chicken breast, place it in a pan with 1 tablespoon lemon juice and just enough water to cover. Season to taste with salt and pepper and poach gently for 10 minutes, or until cooked.

1 Place the chicken, spinach, prosciutto, and shallot in a food processor and process until chopped and blended. Transfer to a bowl, stir in 2 tablespoons of the cheese, the nutmeg, and half the egg. Season with salt and pepper.

2 Halve the Pasta Dough. Wrap one piece in plastic wrap and thinly roll out the other on a lightly floured counter. Cover with a dish towel and roll out the second piece of dough. Place small mounds of the filling in rows 1½ inches/4 cm apart on one sheet of dough and brush the spaces in between with beaten egg. Lift the second piece of dough to fit on top. Press down firmly between the mounds of filling, pushing out any air. Cut into squares and place on a floured dish towel. Let the ravioli rest for 1 hour.

3 Bring a large pan of lightly salted water to a boil. Add the ravioli in batches, return to a boil, and cook for 5 minutes. Remove with a slotted spoon and drain on paper towels, then transfer to a warmed dish.

4 Meanwhile, pour the cream into a skillet, add the garlic and bring to a boil. Let simmer for 1 minute, then add the mushrooms and 2 tablespoons of the remaining cheese. Season to taste and let simmer for 3 minutes. Stir in the basil, then pour the sauce over the ravioli. Sprinkle with the remaining cheese, garnish with basil sprigs, and serve.

chicken & bacon tortellini

serves 6   **prep: 30 mins** ⌕   **cook: 20–30 mins** ⌕

Serve these little stuffed pasta bites plain, sprinkled with Parmesan, or with a sauce of your choice, such as Neapolitan (see page 200), exotic mushrooms (see page 116), or pesto (see page 46).

INGREDIENTS

1 tbsp butter

4 oz/115 g skinless, boneless chicken breast, diced

4 oz/115 g pork fillet, diced

4 oz/115 g pancetta or rindless lean bacon, diced

2 oz/55 g mortadella sausage, coarsely chopped

1 cup freshly grated Parmesan cheese, plus extra for sprinkling

2 eggs, lightly beaten

pinch of ground allspice

salt and pepper

2 quantities Basic Pasta Dough (see page 13)

all-purpose flour, for dusting

variation

If you like, serve the tortellini with a side dish of chopped fresh tomatoes, garnished with fresh basil sprigs.

cook's tip

When working with fresh pasta dough, always make sure that any dough you are not using is covered or wrapped in plastic wrap to prevent it drying out.

1 Melt the butter in a large heavy-bottom skillet. Add the chicken, pork, and pancetta and cook over medium heat, stirring frequently, until lightly browned all over. Remove from the skillet and let cool slightly, then transfer to a food processor. Add the mortadella sausage, Parmesan cheese, and half the eggs, and process

until chopped and blended. Scrape the mixture into a large bowl and season to taste with the allspice, salt, and pepper.

2 Halve the Pasta Dough. Wrap one piece in plastic wrap and roll out the other on a lightly floured counter or cutting board to ½ inch/1 cm thick. Cover with a dish towel and roll out the

second piece of dough. Stamp out circles with a 2-inch/5-cm pastry cutter.

3 Put a small mound of filling in the center of each circle and brush the edges with beaten egg. Fold the circles in half to make semicircles, then fold them round the tip of your index finger and press the ends

together. Bring a large pan of lightly salted water to a boil. Add the tortellini in batches, return to a boil, and cook for 10 minutes. Remove with a slotted spoon and drain on paper towels, then transfer to a warmed serving dish. Sprinkle the tortellini with the extra grated Parmesan cheese and serve immediately.

fruity chicken fusilli

⏲ **cook: 35 mins**

⏱ **prep: 15 mins, plus 30 mins marinating**

serves 4

In this delicious, summery dish, the flavor of the chicken is enhanced by the addition of juicy cubes of mango and a range of exotic spices.

INGREDIENTS

1 lb/450 g skinless, boneless chicken, diced

1 tsp ground turmeric

¼ tsp ground cinnamon

¼ tsp ground cumin

¼ tsp ground cardamom

pinch of cayenne pepper

2 tbsp peanut oil

1 onion, finely chopped

2 garlic cloves, finely chopped

1½ cups Chicken Stock (see page 12)

salt

2 tbsp raisins

1 ripe mango, peeled, seeded, and diced

10 oz/280 g dried fusilli

2 tbsp chopped fresh cilantro, to garnish

variation

Substitute the mango with a ripe papaya, peeled, seeded, and diced, and replace the raisins with the same amount of golden raisins.

cook's tip

You can use meat from the breast, thighs, or drumsticks for this dish. Cooking the chicken first ensures that all the flavors are sealed in.

1 Place the chicken in a shallow dish. Sprinkle with the turmeric, cinnamon, cumin, cardamom, and cayenne and toss well to coat. Cover with plastic wrap and let stand in the refrigerator for 30 minutes.

2 Heat the peanut oil in a heavy-bottom skillet. Add the onion and garlic and cook over low heat, stirring occasionally, for 5 minutes, or until softened. Add the spiced chicken and cook, stirring frequently, for 5 minutes, or until golden brown all over. Pour in the Chicken Stock and season to taste with salt. Bring to a boil, add the raisins and mango, partially cover, and let simmer for 25 minutes.

3 Meanwhile, bring a large heavy-bottom pan of lightly salted water to a boil. Add the pasta, return to a boil, and cook for 8–10 minutes, or until tender but still firm to the bite. Drain and transfer to a warmed serving dish. Add the chicken mixture, toss lightly, and serve, garnished with the cilantro.

pappardelle with chicken & porcini

serves 4   **prep: 15 mins, plus 20 mins soaking**   **cook: 50 mins**

Porcini mushrooms, also known as cèpes, have a wonderful rich, deep flavor. They dry very successfully, remaining redolent of the countryside when reconstituted in hot water.

INGREDIENTS

⅜ cup dried porcini mushrooms

¾ cup hot water

1 lb 12 oz/800 g canned chopped tomatoes

1 fresh red chile, seeded and finely chopped

3 tbsp olive oil

12 oz/350 g skinless, boneless chicken, cut into thin strips

2 garlic cloves, finely chopped

12 oz/350 g dried pappardelle

salt and pepper

2 tbsp chopped fresh flatleaf parsley, to garnish

NUTRITIONAL INFORMATION

Calories	.540
Protein	.33g
Carbohydrate	.78g
Sugars	.9g
Fat	.13g
Saturates	.2g

cook's tip

Exotic mushrooms are used extensively in Italian dishes and porcini mushrooms are the most popular. When using porcini, always soak them first in warm water for 30 minutes, then drain well before cooking.

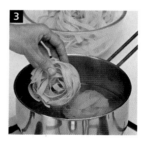

1 Place the porcini in a small bowl, add the hot water, and let soak for 20 minutes. Meanwhile, place the tomatoes and their can juices in a heavy-bottom pan and break them up with a wooden spoon, then stir in the chile. Bring to a boil, reduce the heat, and let simmer, stirring occasionally, for 30 minutes, or until reduced.

2 Remove the mushrooms from their soaking liquid with a slotted spoon, reserving the liquid. Strain the liquid through a coffee filter paper or cheesecloth-lined strainer into the tomatoes and let simmer for an additional 15 minutes. Meanwhile, heat 2 tablespoons of the olive oil in a heavy-bottom skillet. Add the chicken and cook, stirring

frequently, until golden brown all over and tender. Stir in the mushrooms and garlic and cook for 5 minutes.

3 While the chicken is cooking, bring a large heavy-bottom pan of lightly salted water to a boil. Add the pasta, return to a boil, and cook for 8–10 minutes, or until tender but still firm to

the bite. Drain well, transfer to a warmed serving dish, drizzle with the remaining olive oil, and toss lightly. Stir the chicken mixture into the tomato sauce, season to taste with salt and pepper, and spoon onto the pasta. Toss lightly, sprinkle with parsley, and serve immediately.

curried chicken fusilli

cook: 25 mins   **prep: 15 mins**   **serves 4**

This is a good way to use up leftover roast chicken and is an easy, but tasty dish for a midweek supper. Other types of pasta would also work well in this dish, such as farfalle, penne, or conchiglie.

NUTRITIONAL INFORMATION	
Calories	.600
Protein	.47g
Carbohydrate	.54g
Sugars	.3g
Fat	.23g
Saturates	.8g

INGREDIENTS

2 tbsp butter

scant ¼ cup all-purpose flour

scant 2 cups Chicken Stock
(see page 12)

1 tbsp curry paste

6 oz/175 g mushrooms, sliced

1 lb/450 g cooked chicken, ground

salt and pepper

½ cup silvered almonds

9 oz/250 g dried fusilli bucati

4 tbsp light sour cream

cook's tip

You can dice the chicken finely if you do not have a grinder or food processor. When cooking the almonds, keep a close watch on them as they can easily burn.

1 Melt the butter in a heavy-bottom pan. Sprinkle in the flour and cook, stirring constantly, for 1 minute. Remove the pan from the heat and gradually whisk in the Chicken Stock. Return the pan to the heat, stir in the curry paste and bring to a boil, whisking constantly. Add the mushrooms and chicken, season to taste with salt and pepper, reduce the heat, and let simmer gently for 15 minutes.

2 Meanwhile, dry-fry the almonds in a heavy-bottom skillet over low heat, stirring frequently, until golden. Bring a large heavy-bottom pan of lightly salted water to a boil. Add the pasta, return to a boil and cook for 8–10 minutes, or until tender but still firm to the bite. Drain well, then transfer to a warmed serving dish.

3 Stir the sour cream into the chicken mixture and heat through for 1 minute. Spoon the curried chicken onto the pasta, toss lightly, and serve, garnished with the toasted almonds.

fettuccine with two sauces

serves 4   **prep: 20 mins** ⌫   **cook: 30 mins** ⏲

This pretty dish is the perfect choice for a dinner party—and it tastes as delicious as it looks. For an even more striking effect, use tomato, spinach, exotic mushroom, or beet pasta rather than plain.

INGREDIENTS

9 oz/250 g dried fettuccine

salt

fresh basil sprigs, to garnish

RED SAUCE

2 tbsp olive oil

2 shallots, chopped

1 garlic clove, chopped

14 oz/400 g canned chopped tomatoes

2 tbsp shredded fresh basil

2 bay leaves

2 tbsp tomato paste

1 tsp sugar

salt and pepper

WHITE SAUCE

4 tbsp butter

14 oz/400 g skinless, boneless chicken breasts, cut into thin strips

scant ⅞ cup slivered almonds

1¼ cups heavy cream or panna da cucina

salt and pepper

NUTRITIONAL INFORMATION	
Calories 1000	
Protein 37g	
Carbohydrate 57g	
Sugars 11g	
Fat 71g	
Saturates 33g	

variation

Replace the tomato paste with the same amount of sun-dried tomato paste and use fresh tomatoes, peeled and chopped, instead of canned ones.

cook's tip

If possible, always use fresh herbs, as they have a much better flavor than dried. If fresh are unavailable, use freeze-dried herbs instead, which can be found in most large supermarkets.

1 To make the red sauce, heat the olive oil in a heavy-bottom pan. Add the shallots and cook over low heat, stirring occasionally, for 5 minutes. Add the garlic and cook for an additional 1 minute. Stir in the tomatoes, basil, bay leaves, tomato paste, and sugar, and season to taste with salt and pepper. Bring the mixture to a boil, then reduce the heat and let simmer for 20 minutes, or until reduced by half.

2 Meanwhile, make the chicken sauce. Melt the butter in a skillet, add the chicken and almonds and cook over medium heat, stirring constantly, for 5–6 minutes, or until the chicken is browned all over and tender. Pour the cream into a small pan and bring to a boil. Reduce the heat to low and cook for 10 minutes, or until reduced by half. Stir the cream into the chicken mixture and season to taste with salt and pepper.

3 While the white sauce is cooking, bring a large heavy-bottom pan of lightly salted water to a boil.

Add the pasta, return to a boil, and cook for 8–10 minutes, or until tender but still firm to the bite. Drain well and transfer to a warmed serving platter. Remove the bay leaves from the red sauce and spoon it along each side of the platter. Spoon the white sauce along the center. Garnish with basil sprigs and serve.

pasta & chicken medley

serves 2 **prep: 30 mins** ⏲ **cook: 10 mins** ⏲

Strips of cooked chicken are tossed with colored pasta, grapes, and carrot sticks in a delicious pesto-flavored dressing.

INGREDIENTS

4½–5½ oz/125–150 g dried pasta
shapes, such as fusilli
2 tbsp mayonnaise
2 tsp bottled pesto sauce
1 tbsp sour cream
salt and pepper
6 oz/175 g cooked skinless,
boneless chicken
1–2 celery stalks

1 large carrot
1 cup black grapes
(preferably seedless)
celery leaves, to garnish

FRENCH DRESSING
1 tbsp wine vinegar
3 tbsp extra virgin olive oil
salt and pepper

variation

You can replace the sour cream with the same amount of plain yogurt, if you prefer.

cook's tip

To make mayonnaise, mix
1 egg yolk, ½ teaspoon of
dried mustard, salt, pepper,
and ½ teaspoon of sugar.
Gradually stir in ⅔ cup olive oil,
then add 1 tablespoon of wine
vinegar. Use as required.

1 To make the French Dressing, whisk all the ingredients together in a pitcher until smooth.

2 Bring a large, heavy-bottom pan of lightly salted water to a boil. Add the pasta, return to a boil and cook for 8–10 minutes, or until just tender but still firm to the bite. Drain thoroughly, rinse,

and drain again. Transfer to a bowl and mix in 1 tablespoon of the French dressing while hot. Let stand until cold.

3 Mix the mayonnaise, pesto sauce, and sour cream together in a bowl, and season to taste with salt and pepper. Cut the chicken into narrow strips. Cut the celery diagonally into narrow slices.

Reserve a few grapes for the garnish, halve the rest, and remove any pips. Cut the carrot into julienne strips.

4 Add the chicken, celery, carrot, the halved grapes, and the mayonnaise mixture to the pasta, and toss thoroughly. Taste and adjust the seasoning, if necessary.

Arrange the pasta mixture in 2 serving dishes and garnish with the reserved black grapes and the celery leaves.

garganelli with chicken & feta

serves 4 | **prep: 10 mins** | **cook: 10 mins**

This unusual combination makes a simple and enjoyable midweek supper that is just right for warm summer evenings.

INGREDIENTS

2 tbsp olive oil

1 lb/450 g skinless, boneless chicken breasts, cut into thin strips

6 scallions, chopped

8 oz/225 g feta cheese, diced

4 tbsp chopped fresh chives

salt and pepper

1 lb/450 g dried garganelli

NUTRITIONAL INFORMATION	
Calories	700
Protein	48g
Carbohydrate	84g
Sugars	4g
Fat	22g
Saturates	2g

variation

Substitute diced, firm, white fish fillet such as angler fish for the chicken and replace the garganelli with either penne or pipe rigate, if you like.

1 Heat the olive oil in a heavy-bottom skillet. Add the chicken and cook over medium heat, stirring frequently, for 5–8 minutes, or until golden all over and cooked through. Add the scallions and cook for 2 minutes. Stir the feta cheese into the skillet with half the chives and season to taste with salt and pepper.

2 Meanwhile, bring a large heavy-bottom pan of lightly salted water to a boil. Add the pasta, return to a boil, and cook for 8–10 minutes, or until tender but still firm to the bite. Drain well, then transfer to a warmed serving dish.

3 Spoon the chicken mixture onto the pasta, toss lightly, and serve immediately, garnished with the remaining chives.

tuscan chicken tagliarini

cook: 45 mins   **prep: 15 mins**   **serves 4**

Simplicity is the keynote of Tuscan cuisine—and this means using the best and freshest ingredients for a memorable meal.

NUTRITIONAL INFORMATION	
Calories	.570
Protein	.40g
Carbohydrate	.76g
Sugars	.10g
Fat	.11g
Saturates	.2g

INGREDIENTS

2 tbsp olive oil

4 skinless, boneless chicken breasts

1 onion, thinly sliced

2 red bell peppers, seeded and sliced

1 garlic clove, finely chopped

1¼ cups strained tomatoes

⅔ cup dry white wine

1 tbsp chopped fresh marjoram

salt and pepper

12 oz/350 g dried tagliarini

14 oz/400 g canned cannellini beans, drained and rinsed

variation

Use 1 lb/450 g shelled raw shrimp instead of chicken. Cook them in oil in Step 1 until they turn pink; set aside. Return to the pan with the beans in Step 3.

1 Heat half the olive oil in a heavy-bottom skillet. Add the chicken and cook over medium heat for 4 minutes, or until golden brown on all sides. Remove from the skillet and keep warm. Reduce the heat, add the onion and red bell peppers to the skillet and cook, stirring occasionally, for 5 minutes, or until softened. Stir in the garlic. Return the chicken to the skillet, add the strained tomatoes, wine, and marjoram, and season to taste with salt and pepper. Cover and let simmer gently, stirring occasionally, for 30 minutes, or until the chicken is tender.

2 Meanwhile, bring a large heavy-bottom pan of lightly salted water to a boil. Add the pasta, return to a boil, and cook for 8–10 minutes, or until tender but still firm to the bite. Drain well, return to the pan, drizzle with the remaining oil, and toss lightly.

3 Stir the cannellini beans into the chicken mixture and let simmer for 5 minutes, or until heated through. Divide the pasta between serving plates and top with the sauce.

penne with chicken & arugula

serves 4   **prep: 15 mins**   **cook: 25 mins**

*The sharp, peppery flavor of arugula contrasts with the creamy
richness of the sauce in this aromatic dish.*

INGREDIENTS

2 tbsp butter

2 carrots, cut into thin sticks

1 small onion, finely chopped

8 oz/225 g skinless, boneless

chicken breast, diced

8 oz/225 g mushrooms, quartered

½ cup dry white wine

½ cup Chicken Stock

(see page 12)

2 garlic cloves, finely chopped

salt and pepper

2 tbsp cornstarch

4 tbsp water

2 tbsp light cream

½ cup plain yogurt

2 tsp fresh thyme leaves

2½ cups arugula

12 oz/350 g dried penne

fresh thyme sprigs, to garnish

NUTRITIONAL INFORMATION	
Calories	.555
Protein	.27g
Carbohydrate	.87g
Sugars	.10g
Fat	.11g
Saturates	.5g

variation

Replace the arugula with the same
amount of fresh watercress or baby
spinach leaves, if you prefer.

cook's tip

For a meatier dish, use chicken
or turkey thighs and cook for
slightly longer, until the meat is
thoroughly cooked through.
If you prefer a strong garlic
flavor, then finely slice the
garlic instead of chopping it.

1 Melt the butter in a
heavy-bottom skillet.
Add the carrots and cook over
medium heat, stirring
frequently, for 2 minutes.
Add the onion, chicken,
mushrooms, wine, Chicken
Stock, and garlic, and season
to taste with salt and pepper.
Mix the cornstarch and water
together in a bowl until a
smooth paste forms, then stir

in the cream and yogurt. Stir
the cornstarch mixture into the
skillet with the thyme, cover,
and let simmer for 5 minutes.
Place the arugula on top of the
chicken, but do not stir in,
cover and cook for 5 minutes,
or until the chicken is tender.

2 Strain the cooking
liquid into a clean pan,
then transfer the chicken and

vegetables to a dish and keep
warm. Heat the cooking
liquid, whisking occasionally,
for 10 minutes, or until
reduced and thickened.

3 Meanwhile, bring a
large heavy-bottom
pan of lightly salted water
to a boil. Add the pasta,
return to a boil and cook for
8–10 minutes, or until tender

but still firm to the bite. Return
the chicken and vegetables to
the thickened cooking liquid
and stir to coat.

4 Drain the pasta well,
transfer to a warmed
serving dish, and spoon the
chicken and vegetable mixture
on top. Garnish with thyme
sprigs and serve immediately.

marsala mushroom lasagna

serves 4   **prep: 40 mins** ⟳   **cook: 1 hr 45 mins** ⟳

You can use your favorite mushrooms, such as chanterelles or oyster mushrooms, for this delicately flavored dish.

INGREDIENTS

butter, for greasing

14 sheets precooked lasagna

3½ cups Béchamel Sauce (see page 12)

¾ cup grated Parmesan cheese

EXOTIC MUSHROOM SAUCE

2 tbsp olive oil

2 garlic cloves, crushed

1 large onion, finely chopped

8 oz/225 g exotic mushrooms, sliced

generous 1¼ cups fresh ground chicken

3 oz/75 g chicken livers, finely chopped

4 oz/115 g prosciutto, diced

⅔ cup Marsala wine

10 oz/285 g canned chopped tomatoes

1 tbsp chopped fresh basil leaves

2 tbsp tomato paste

salt and pepper

NUTRITIONAL INFORMATION

Calories	.708
Protein	.35g
Carbohydrates	.57g
Sugars	.17g
Fat	.35g
Saturates	.14g

variation

Replace the chopped fresh basil with the same amount of fresh flatleaf parsley, if you like.

cook's tip

There are many different types of exotic mushrooms available, including morels, chanterelles, and portobello mushrooms. To prepare, wipe the portobello mushrooms with a damp cloth and rinse the rest in cold water.

1 Preheat the oven to 375°F/190°C. To make the sauce, heat the olive oil in a large, heavy-bottom pan. Add the garlic, onion, and mushrooms, and cook, stirring frequently, for an additional 6 minutes. Add the ground chicken, chicken livers, and prosciutto, and cook over low heat for 12 minutes, or until the meat has browned.

2 Stir the Marsala, tomatoes, basil, and tomato paste into the mixture, and cook for 4 minutes. Season to taste with salt and pepper, cover, and let simmer for 30 minutes. Uncover, stir, and simmer for 15 minutes.

3 Lightly grease an ovenproof dish with butter. Arrange sheets of lasagna over the base of the dish, spoon over a layer of the exotic mushroom sauce, then spoon over a layer of Béchamel Sauce. Place another layer of lasagna on top and repeat the process twice, finishing with a layer of Béchamel Sauce. Sprinkle over the grated cheese and bake in the preheated oven for 35 minutes, or until golden brown and bubbling. Serve immediately.

chicken tortellini

serves 4   **prep: 1 hr**   **cook: 35 mins**

Impress your guests with hand-made, fresh tortellini filled with a delicious blend of Italian flavors and served with a creamy Parmesan and mushroom sauce.

INGREDIENTS

4 oz/115 g boned chicken
breast, skinned

2 oz/55 g prosciutto

1½ oz/40 g cooked spinach,
well drained

1 tbsp finely chopped onion

2 tbsp freshly grated Parmesan cheese

pinch of ground allspice

1 egg, beaten

1 lb/450 g basic pasta dough
(see page 13)

salt and pepper

2 tbsp chopped fresh parsley,
to garnish

SAUCE

1¼ cups light cream

2 garlic cloves, crushed

4 oz/115 g white mushrooms,
thinly sliced

4 tbsp freshly grated Parmesan cheese

NUTRITIONAL INFORMATION	
Calories	.635
Protein	.31g
Carbohydrate	.50g
Sugars	.4g
Fat	.36g
Saturates	.16g

variation

For a low-fat sauce substitute low-fat yogurt for the cream, omit the Parmesan cheese, and stir in finely chopped basil.

cook's tip

Think ahead by making double the quantity of filled tortellini. What you don't use will keep in the refrigerator for up to 3 days and can be used for a quick mid-week supper or snack.

1 Bring a pan of salted water to a boil. Add the chicken and poach for about 10 minutes. Let cool slightly, then place in a food processor with the prosciutto, spinach, and onion and process until finely chopped. Stir in the Parmesan cheese, allspice, and egg and season with salt and pepper to taste.

2 Thinly roll out the pasta dough and cut into 1½–2-inch/4–5-cm circles.

3 Place ½ teaspoon of the chicken and ham filling in the center of each circle. Fold the pieces in half and press the edges to seal, then wrap each piece round your index finger, cross over the ends, and curl the rest of the dough backward to make a navel shape. Re-roll the trimmings and repeat until all of the dough is used up.

4 Bring a pan of salted water to a boil. Add the tortellini, in batches, return to a boil and cook for 5 minutes. Drain the tortellini well and transfer to a serving dish.

5 To make the sauce, bring the cream and garlic to a boil in a small pan, then simmer for 3 minutes. Add the mushrooms and half of the cheese, season to taste with salt and pepper, and simmer for 2–3 minutes. Pour the sauce over the tortellini. Sprinkle over the remaining Parmesan cheese, garnish with the parsley, and serve.

pheasant lasagna

serves 4   **prep: 40 mins** ⏲   **cook: 1 hr 15 mins** ⏲

This scrumptious and unusual baked lasagna is virtually a meal in itself. It is served with baby onions and green peas.

INGREDIENTS

butter, for greasing

14 sheets precooked lasagna

3½ cups Béchamel Sauce (see page 12)

¾ cup grated mozzarella cheese

FILLING

8 oz/225 g bacon fat, diced

2 oz/55 g butter

16 small onions

8 large pheasant breasts, thinly sliced

3½ tbsp plain flour

2½ cups Chicken Stock (see page 12)

1 bouquet garni

1 lb/450 g fresh peas, shelled

salt and pepper

NUTRITIONAL INFORMATION

Calories	1038
Protein	...............65g
Carbohydrate	..........54g
Sugars	...............13g
Fat	..................64g
Saturates	.............27g

variation

Frozen peas would also work well in this recipe. Substitute shallots for the small onions, if you prefer.

cook's tip

There are 2 types of mozzarella cheese, buffalo and cow's milk. In Italy, buffalo milk mozzarella is usually eaten raw because it has a very delicate flavor while the cow's milk variety is used in cooking.

1 Preheat the oven to 400°F/200°C. To make the filling, place the bacon fat into a pan of boiling, salted water and simmer for 3 minutes, then drain and pat dry. Melt the butter in a large skillet. Add the bacon fat and onions and cook for 3 minutes, or until lightly browned. Remove the bacon fat and onions from the skillet and reserve. Add the slices of pheasant and cook over low heat for 12 minutes, or until browned all over. Transfer to an ovenproof dish.

2 Stir the flour into the skillet and cook until just brown, then blend in the stock. Pour the mixture over the pheasant, add the bouquet garni, and cook in the oven for 5 minutes. Remove the bouquet garni. Add the onions, bacon fat, and peas and return to the oven for 10 minutes. Place the pheasant and bacon fat in a food processor and grind finely.

3 Reduce the oven temperature to 375°F/190°C. Grease an ovenproof dish with butter.

Make layers of lasagna, pheasant sauce, and Béchamel Sauce in the dish, ending with Béchamel Sauce. Sprinkle over the cheese and bake for 30 minutes, or until golden and bubbling. Serve.

slices of duckling with pasta

serves 4 **prep: 15 mins** **cook: 25 mins**

A raspberry and honey sauce superbly counterbalances the richness of the duckling in this recipe.

INGREDIENTS

4 boned breasts of duckling (about 9 oz/275 g each)

salt and pepper

2 tbsp butter

1/2 cup finely chopped carrots

1/2 cup finely chopped shallots

1 tbsp lemon juice

2/3 cup Chicken Stock (see page 12)

4 tbsp honey

3/4 cup fresh or thawed frozen raspberries

3 1/2 tbsp all-purpose flour

1 tbsp Worcestershire sauce

14 oz/400 g fresh linguine

TO GARNISH

fresh raspberries

fresh flatleaf parsley sprigs

NUTRITIONAL INFORMATION

Calories 686

Protein 62g

Carbohydrate 70g

Sugars 15g

Fat 20g

Saturates 7g

variation

You can use another meat stock and use other types of fresh pasta, such as spaghetti or tagliatelle, if you prefer.

cook's tip

Scoring the duck breasts helps to release the fat during cooking. Ducklings are usually available all year round. Look for ones that have a supple skin and a plump breast.

1 Trim and score the duck breasts with a sharp knife and season well all over. Melt the butter in a skillet, add the duck breasts, and cook all over until lightly colored. Add the carrots, shallots, lemon juice, and half the stock, and simmer over low heat for 1 minute. Stir in half of the honey and half of the raspberries. Sprinkle over half of the flour and cook, stirring, for 3 minutes. Season with pepper to taste and add the Worcestershire sauce.

2 Stir in the remaining stock and cook for 1 minute. Stir in the remaining honey and raspberries, and sprinkle over the remaining flour. Cook for an additional 3 minutes.

3 Remove the duck breasts from the skillet, but let the sauce continue simmering over very low heat.

4 Meanwhile, bring a large, heavy-bottom pan of lightly salted water to a boil. Add the linguine, return to a boil and cook for 8–10 minutes, or until tender but still firm to the bite. Drain and divide between 4 individual plates.

5 Slice the duck breast lengthwise into 1/4-inch/5-mm-thick pieces. Pour a little sauce over the pasta and arrange the sliced duck in a fan shape on top of it. Garnish with raspberries and parsley and serve immediately.

fish & shellfish

We are advised by nutritionists to eat more fish—at least two meals a week—and what better way is there to enjoy it than in combination with pasta? Even fussy children, who would not contemplate tackling a fish fillet on its own, will tuck into Haddock & Pasta Bake (see page 141) or Lasagna alla Marinara (see page 136), and they may even surprise you with a new-found enthusiasm for squid or clams. Shellfish have an affinity with pasta, and mussels, clams, scallops, and shrimp feature in many classic recipes, such as Fettuccine with Saffron Mussels (see page 159) and Spaghetti con Vongole (see page 162).

The versatility of pasta is matched by the versatility of fish and shellfish, providing endless scope for marvelous meals. Recipes range from quick and easy pantry dishes, such as Spaghettini with Quick Tuna Sauce (see page 130), to the time-consuming but truly wonderful Crab Ravioli (see page 152), and from the cheap and cheerful Linguine with Sardines (see page 128) to the utterly outrageous Spaghetti with Shrimp & Caviar (see page 167). As well as fabulous fish sauces served with long or short pasta and substantial layered bakes, you will find unusual pasta packages and even a Pasta Omelet with Shrimp (see page 165). Whatever the occasion or time of year, pasta with seafood will provide a nourishing, satisfying and, above all, delicious meal.

pasta pudding

serves 4   **prep: 35 mins**   **cook: 2 hrs**

A tasty mixture of creamy fish and pasta cooked in a bowl, presents macaroni in a new guise. It is delicious served with a fresh tomato salad or tomato sauce.

INGREDIENTS

4½ oz/125 g dried short-cut macaroni, or other short pasta shapes

1 tbsp butter, plus extra for greasing

1 lb 2 oz/500 g white fish fillets, such as cod or haddock

few fresh parsley stalks

6 black peppercorns

½ cup heavy cream

2 eggs, separated

2 tbsp chopped fresh dill

pinch of grated nutmeg

½ cup freshly grated Parmesan cheese

pepper

fresh tomato salad or sauce, to serve

fresh dill sprigs, to garnish

NUTRITIONAL INFORMATION	
Calories 536
Protein 35g
Carbohydrate 21g
Sugars 4g
Fat 35g
Saturates 17g

variation

Replace the fresh dill with the same amount of fresh flatleaf parsley, if you prefer.

cook's tip

Always whisk egg whites in a spotlessly clean, dry bowl, which is free from any grease, otherwise they will not hold their shape very well.

1 Bring a large pan of lightly salted water to a boil. Add the pasta, return to a boil, and cook for 8–10 minutes. Drain, return to the pan, add the butter and cover. Keep warm.

2 Place the fish in a skillet with the parsley and peppercorns and pour on just enough water to cover. Bring to a boil, cover, and simmer for 10 minutes. Lift out the fish, reserving the liquor. When the fish is cool enough to handle, skin and remove any bones. Cut into bite-size pieces. Transfer the pasta to a bowl and stir in the cream, egg yolks, and dill. Stir in the fish, taking care not to break it up, and enough liquor to make a moist but firm mixture. It should not be too runny. Whisk the egg whites until stiff but not dry, then fold into the mixture. Grease a heatproof pudding bowl and spoon in the mixture to within 1½ inch/4 cm of the rim. Cover the top with greased waxed paper and a cloth, or with foil, and tie around the rim. Do not use foil if you cook in a microwave.

3 Stand the pudding on a trivet in a pan of boiling water to come halfway up the sides. Cover and steam for 1½ hours, topping up the boiling water, or cook in a microwave on HIGH power for 7 minutes. Run a knife round the inside of the bowl and invert into a dish. Garnish with dill and serve.

linguine with sardines

serves 4 **prep: 10 mins** **cook: 20 mins**

Quick and easy, yet packed full of flavor, this pasta dish can be made entirely from pantry ingredients for a midweek supper when you have been too busy to think about planning the meal.

INGREDIENTS

4 tbsp olive oil

1 small onion, finely chopped

2 oz/55 g canned anchovy
fillets, drained

14 oz/400 g canned chopped tomatoes

¼ cup pine nuts

9 oz/250 g canned sardines in
oil, drained

salt and pepper

12 oz/350 g dried linguine

½ cup dried, uncolored bread crumbs

NUTRITIONAL INFORMATION

Calories 655

Protein 29g

Carbohydrate 80g

Sugars 8g

Fat 27g

Saturates 3g

cook's tip

If you have any fresh herbs, such as flatleaf parsley or thyme, chop 1–2 tablespoons and add with the bread crumbs in Step 3.

1 Heat the olive oil in a large, heavy-bottom skillet. Add the onion and anchovies and cook over low heat, stirring occasionally, for 5 minutes, or until the onion has softened. Add the pine nuts and tomatoes and let simmer for 10 minutes. Add the sardines, season to taste with salt and pepper, and let simmer for 5 minutes.

2 Meanwhile, bring a large, heavy-bottom pan of lightly salted water to a boil. Add the pasta, return to a boil, and cook for 8–10 minutes, or until tender but still firm to the bite.

3 Drain the pasta well, transfer to a large, warmed serving dish and add the sardine mixture and the bread crumbs. Toss lightly and serve immediately.

mafalde with fresh salmon

cook: 25 mins   **prep: 15 mins**   **serves 4**

While this creamy combination of fresh salmon and shrimp may seem quite extravagant, a little goes a long way. This dish is perfect for an informal dinner party, if served with a crisp green salad.

NUTRITIONAL INFORMATION	
Calories	.716
Protein	.35g
Carbohydrate	.70g
Sugars	.8g
Fat	.31g
Saturates	.13g

INGREDIENTS

12 oz/350 g salmon fillet

fresh dill sprigs, plus extra to garnish

1 cup dry white wine

salt and pepper

6 tomatoes, peeled and chopped

⅔ cup heavy cream or panna da cucina

12 oz/350 g dried mafalde

4 oz/115 g cooked, shelled shrimp

cook's tip

If using frozen shrimp, make sure that they are completely thawed before using. If you are unable to find mafalde pasta, then use pappardelle instead.

1 Place the salmon in a large heavy-bottom skillet. Add a few dill sprigs, pour in the wine, and season to taste with salt and pepper. Bring to a boil, then reduce the heat, cover, and poach gently for 5 minutes, or until the flesh flakes easily. Remove with a spatula, reserving the cooking liquid, and let cool slightly. Remove and discard the skin and any remaining small bones, then flake the flesh into large chunks.

2 Add the tomatoes and cream to the reserved liquid. Bring to a boil, then reduce the heat and simmer for 15 minutes, or until thickened.

3 Meanwhile, bring a large heavy-bottom pan of lightly salted water to a boil. Add the pasta, return to a boil, and cook for 8–10 minutes, or until tender but still firm to the bite. Drain and transfer to a warmed serving dish.

4 Add the salmon and shrimp to the tomato mixture and stir gently until coated in the sauce. Spoon the salmon sauce onto the pasta, toss lightly, then serve, garnished with dill sprigs.

spaghettini with quick tuna sauce

serves 4 **prep: 20 mins** **cook: 30 mins**

Canned fish is such a useful and versatile ingredient. Here, canned tuna is combined with fresh tomatoes, mushrooms, and herbs to make a scrumptious pasta sauce.

INGREDIENTS

3 tbsp olive oil

4 tomatoes, peeled, seeded, and coarsely chopped

4 oz/115 g mushrooms, sliced

1 tbsp shredded fresh basil

14 oz/400 g canned tuna, drained

generous ⅓ cup Fish Stock or Chicken Stock (see page 12)

1 garlic clove, finely chopped

2 tsp chopped fresh marjoram

salt and pepper

12 oz/350 g dried spaghettini

1 cup freshly grated Parmesan cheese, to serve

NUTRITIONAL INFORMATION

Calories 600

Protein 35g

Carbohydrate 68g

Sugars 6g

Fat 24g

Saturates 8g

variation

Use other canned fish such as salmon instead of the tuna, and replace the shredded fresh basil with the same amount of finely chopped fresh parsley.

cook's tip

If fresh ingredients are limited, use 14 oz/400 g canned tomatoes and a low-salt bouillon cube. You could also substitute 1 teaspoon chopped preserved garlic or a pinch of garlic powder for the fresh clove.

1 Heat the olive oil in a large skillet. Add the tomatoes and cook over low heat, stirring occasionally, for 15 minutes, or until pulpy. Add the mushrooms and cook, stirring occasionally, for an additional 10 minutes. Stir in the basil, tuna, Fish Stock, garlic, and marjoram, and season to taste with salt and pepper. Cook over low heat for 5 minutes, or until heated through.

2 Meanwhile, bring a large heavy-bottom pan of lightly salted water to a boil. Add the pasta, return to a boil, and cook for 8–10 minutes, or until tender but still firm to the bite.

3 Drain the pasta well, transfer to a warmed serving dish, and spoon on the tuna mixture. Serve with grated Parmesan cheese.

spaghetti, tuna & parsley

serves 4   **prep: 10 mins**   **cook: 15 mins**

This is a recipe to look forward to when parsley is at its most prolific, in the growing season.

INGREDIENTS

1 lb 2 oz/500 g dried spaghetti

1 oz/25 g butter

black olives, to serve (optional)

SAUCE

7 oz/200 g canned tuna, drained

2 oz/55 g canned anchovies, drained

1 cup olive oil

generous 1 cup coarsely chopped fresh flatleaf parsley

⅔ cup sour cream or yogurt

salt and pepper

NUTRITIONAL INFORMATION

Calories	.970
Protein	.23g
Carbohydrate	.42g
Sugars	.2g
Fat	.80g
Saturates	.18g

cook's tip

Anchovies can be quite salty. To remove some of the salt, soak the anchovies in a little milk for 20 minutes. Drain, then rinse under cold running water and proceed as in main recipe.

1 Bring a large, heavy-bottom pan of lightly salted water to a boil. Add the spaghetti, return to a boil, and cook for 8–10 minutes, or until tender but still firm to the bite. Drain the spaghetti in a colander and return to the pan. Add the butter, toss thoroughly to coat, and keep warm until required.

2 Flake the tuna into smaller pieces using 2 forks. Place the tuna in a blender or food processor with the anchovies, olive oil, and parsley and process until the sauce is smooth. Pour in the sour cream or yogurt and process for a few seconds to blend. Taste the sauce and season with salt and pepper, if necessary.

3 Warm 4 plates. Shake the pan of spaghetti over medium heat for a few minutes, or until it is thoroughly warmed through.

4 Pour the sauce over the spaghetti and toss quickly, using 2 forks. Serve immediately with a small dish of black olives, if liked.

pasta & sicilian sauce

cook: 30 mins   **prep: 10 mins, plus 20 mins soaking**   **serves 4**

This Sicilian recipe of anchovies mixed with pine nuts and golden raisins in a tomato sauce is delicious with all types of pasta.

NUTRITIONAL INFORMATION	
Calories	.286
Protein	.11g
Carbohydrate	.46g
Sugars	.14g
Fat	.8g
Saturates	.1g

INGREDIENTS

½ cup golden raisins

1 lb/450 g tomatoes, halved

¼ cup pine nuts

1¾ oz/50 g canned anchovies, drained and halved lengthwise

2 tbsp concentrated tomato paste

1 lb 8 oz/675 g fresh or

12 oz/350 g dried penne

variation

Add 3½ oz/100 g bacon, broiled for 5 minutes, or until crispy, then chopped, instead of the anchovies, if you prefer.

1 Preheat the broiler, then cook the tomatoes under the hot broiler for 10 minutes. Let cool slightly, then once cool enough to handle, peel off the skin and dice the flesh. Place the pine nuts on a cookie sheet and lightly toast under the broiler for 2–3 minutes, or until golden brown.

2 Soak the golden raisins in a bowl of warm water for about 20 minutes. Drain them thoroughly.

3 Place the tomatoes, pine nuts and golden raisins in a small pan and heat gently. Add the anchovies and tomato paste, heating the sauce for an additional 2–3 minutes, or until hot.

4 Bring a large, heavy-bottom pan of lightly salted water to a boil. Add the pasta, return to a boil, and cook for 8–10 minutes, or until tender but still firm to the bite. Drain thoroughly, then transfer the pasta to a serving plate and serve with the Sicilian sauce.

fettuccine alla buchaniera

⏱ **cook: 50 mins**   ⏱ **prep: 20 mins**   **serves 6**

This classic, yet simple recipe brings out both the delicate flavor of sole and the more robust taste of angler fish.

variation

You can substitute flounder or dab for the sole fillets and haddock or cod for the angler fish, if you like.

INGREDIENTS

generous ½ cup all-purpose flour	1 carrot, diced
salt and pepper	1 leek, finely chopped
1 lb/450 g lemon sole fillets, skinned	1¼ cups Fish Stock (see page 12)
and cut into chunks	1¼ cups dry white wine
1 lb/450 g angler fish fillets, skinned	2 tsp anchovy essence
and cut into chunks	1 tbsp balsamic vinegar
3 oz/85 g unsalted butter	1 lb/450 g dried fettuccine
4 shallots, finely chopped	chopped fresh flatleaf parsley,
2 garlic cloves, crushed	to garnish

cook's tip

Make sure you remove the gray membrane, as well as the skin, from the angler fish before cooking. The white membrane helps to hold the fish together during cooking.

1 Season the flour with salt and pepper and spread out 2 tablespoons on a plate. Coat all the fish pieces with it, shaking off the excess. Melt the butter in a heavy-bottom pan or flameproof casserole. Add the fish, shallots, garlic, carrot, and leek, then cook over low heat, stirring frequently, for 10 minutes. Sprinkle in the remaining seasoned flour and cook, stirring constantly, for 1 minute.

2 Mix the Fish Stock, wine, anchovy essence, and balsamic vinegar together in a pitcher and gradually stir into the fish mixture. Bring to a boil, stirring constantly, then reduce the heat and let simmer gently for 35 minutes.

3 Meanwhile, bring a large heavy-bottom pan of lightly salted water to a boil. Add the pasta, return to a boil, and cook for 8–10 minutes, or until tender but still firm to the bite. Drain and transfer to a warmed serving dish. Spoon the fish mixture onto the pasta, garnish with chopped parsley, and serve immediately.

lasagna alla marinara

serves 6   **prep: 20 mins** ⏲   **cook: 45 mins** ⏲

This lasagna looks, tastes, and smells wonderful and makes an excellent choice for informal entertaining.

INGREDIENTS

1 tbsp butter	salt and pepper
8 oz/225 g raw shrimp, shelled, deveined, and coarsely chopped	14 oz/400 g canned chopped tomatoes
1 lb/450 g angler fish fillets, skinned and chopped	1 tbsp chopped fresh chervil
	1 tbsp shredded fresh basil
8 oz/225 g cremini mushrooms, chopped	6 oz/175 g dried no-precook lasagna
3½ cups Béchamel Sauce (see page 12)	¾ cup freshly grated Parmesan cheese

NUTRITIONAL INFORMATION

Calories	.500
Protein	.32g
Carbohydrate	.41g
Sugars	.12g
Fat	.24g
Saturates	.15g

variation

If fresh chervil is unavailable, then use tarragon, dill, or parsley instead. Spinach-flavored lasagna would also work well in this dish.

cook's tip

This filling would be ideal to use in dried cannelloni tubes with a sauce of your choice. Cut the fish and shrimp into small pieces, otherwise it may be difficult to fill the tubes.

1 Preheat the oven to 375°F/190°C. Melt the butter in a large heavy-bottom pan. Add the shrimp and angler fish and cook over medium heat for 3–5 minutes, or until the shrimp change color. Transfer the shrimp to a small heatproof bowl with a slotted spoon. Add the mushrooms to the pan and cook, stirring occasionally, for 5 minutes. Transfer the fish and mushrooms to the bowl.

2 Stir the fish mixture, with any juices, into the Béchamel Sauce and season to taste with salt and pepper. Layer the tomatoes, chervil, basil, fish mixture, and lasagna sheets in a large ovenproof dish, ending with a layer of the fish mixture. Sprinkle evenly with the grated Parmesan cheese.

3 Bake in the preheated oven for 35 minutes, or until golden brown, then serve immediately.

italian fish stew with ziti

serves 4 **prep: 20 mins** ⟳ **cook: 20 mins** ⟳

Whether you are entertaining or just cooking for the family, this light and refreshing dish is the perfect meal at any time of the year.

INGREDIENTS

pinch of saffron threads

4 cups Fish Stock (see page 12)

4 tbsp butter

1 lb/450 g red snapper fillets, thinly sliced

12 prepared scallops

12 raw jumbo shrimp, shelled and deveined

8 oz/225 g raw shrimp, shelled and deveined

salt and pepper

finely grated rind and juice of 1 lemon

⅔ cup white wine vinegar

⅔ cup white wine

⅔ cup heavy cream or panna da cucina

3 tbsp chopped fresh flatleaf parsley

1 lb/450 g dried ziti

NUTRITIONAL INFORMATION

Calories	.940
Protein	.63g
Carbohydrate	.88g
Sugars	.5g
Fat	.37g
Saturates	.19g

variation

Replace the red snapper with gray snapper. Other types of pasta would also work well in this dish, such as tortiglioni or campanelle.

cook's tip

Use a mixture of different-sized shrimp for an authentic Italian dish. There are many varieties available in Italy, from the tiny *gamberetti* to *gamberoni*—the Mediterranean equivalent of jumbo shrimp.

1 Place the saffron in a small bowl, add 3 tablespoons of the Fish Stock, and let soak. Melt the butter in a large heavy-bottom pan or flameproof casserole. Add the red snapper, scallops, and both types of shrimp and cook over medium heat, stirring frequently, for 3–5 minutes, or until the shrimp have changed color. Season to taste with

pepper and add the grated rind and lemon juice. Transfer the fish and shellfish to a plate and keep warm.

2 Pour the remaining stock into the pan and add the saffron and its soaking liquid. Bring to a boil and cook until reduced by about one-third. Add the vinegar and continue to boil for 4 minutes.

Stir in the white wine and cook for 5 minutes, or until reduced and thickened. Add the cream and parsley, then season to taste with salt and pepper and let simmer gently for 2 minutes.

3 Meanwhile, bring a large heavy-bottom pan of lightly salted water to a boil. Add the pasta, return to

a boil, and cook for 8–10 minutes, or until tender but still firm to the bite. Drain well and transfer to a large, warmed serving platter. Arrange the fish and shellfish on top and pour over the sauce. Serve immediately.

bavettini with smoked salmon & arugula

serves 4　　　　　**prep: 10 mins** ⏲　　　　　**cook: 10 mins** ⏲

Pasta with attitude—this simple and elegant dish is pure perfection.
Serve with a fresh green salad for a filling lunch.

INGREDIENTS

12 oz/350 g dried bavettini

2 tbsp olive oil

1 garlic clove, finely chopped

4 oz/115 g smoked salmon,
cut into thin strips

1¼ cups arugula

salt and pepper

NUTRITIONAL INFORMATION

Calories	.395
Protein	.18g
Carbohydrate	.65g
Sugars	.3g
Fat	.9g
Saturates	.1g

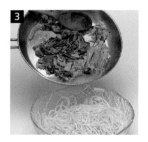

cook's tip

Do not overcook the salmon or arugula; they should just be warmed through and the arugula lightly wilted. If arugula is unavailable, use baby spinach leaves instead.

1 Bring a large heavy-bottom pan of lightly salted water to a boil. Add the pasta, return to a boil, and cook for 8–10 minutes, or until tender but still firm to the bite.

2 Just before the end of the cooking time, heat the olive oil in a heavy-bottom skillet. Add the garlic and cook over low heat, stirring constantly, for 1 minute. Do not let the garlic brown or it will taste bitter. Add the salmon and arugula. Season to taste with pepper and cook, stirring constantly, for 1 minute. Remove the skillet from the heat.

3 Drain the pasta and transfer to a large, warmed serving dish. Add the smoked salmon and arugula mixture, toss lightly, and serve immediately.

haddock & pasta bake

cook: 25 mins   **prep: 20 mins**   **serves 4**

Warming, filling, and comforting, this is just the right dish for a family supper in the middle of winter.

NUTRITIONAL INFORMATION

Calories 787

Protein 44g

Carbohydrate 98g

Sugars 10g

Fat 27g

Saturates 15g

INGREDIENTS

2 tbsp butter, plus extra for greasing

1 lb/450 g smoked haddock fillets, thickly sliced

2½ cups milk

1 bay leaf

4 juniper berries

2 hard-cooked eggs, shelled

scant ¼ cup all-purpose flour

pinch of cayenne pepper

salt and pepper

2 tsp lemon juice

3 tbsp heavy cream

1 tbsp chopped fresh parsley

1 lb/450 g dried elbow macaroni

cook's tip

Look for undyed smoked haddock, which is a more attractive color, has a better flavor, and is healthier. It is usually available in most large supermarkets.

1 Preheat the oven to 400°F/200°C. Grease a large ovenproof dish with butter. Place the fish in the dish, pour in the milk, and add the bay leaf and juniper berries. Cover and bake in the preheated oven for 15 minutes.

2 Just before the fish is cooked, bring a large heavy-bottom pan of lightly salted water to a boil. Add the pasta, then return to a boil, and cook for 8–10 minutes, or until tender but still firm to the bite.

3 Meanwhile, remove the fish from the oven, but do not switch the oven off. Carefully pour the cooking liquid into a measuring cup without breaking up the fish. Remove and discard the bay leaf and juniper berries.

4 Mash the eggs in a bowl with a fork and set aside. Melt the butter in a pan, stir in the flour, and cook, stirring, for 1 minute. Remove from the heat and gradually whisk in the reserved cooking liquid. Return the pan to the heat and season to taste with cayenne, salt, and pepper. Stir in the lemon juice, cream, parsley, and mashed egg, and cook, stirring constantly, for 2 minutes.

5 Drain the pasta and spoon it over the fish. Pour the sauce over the top and bake in the preheated oven for 10 minutes. Serve.

macaroni & seafood bake

serves 4   **prep: 30 mins**   **cook: 50 mins**

This adaptation of an eighteenth-century Italian dish is baked until it is golden brown and sizzling, then cut into wedges like a cake.

INGREDIENTS

12 oz/350 g dried
short-cut macaroni
olive oil, for brushing
3 oz/85 g butter, plus extra
for greasing
2 small fennel bulbs, thinly sliced and
fronds reserved
6 oz/175 g mushrooms, thinly sliced
6 oz/175 g cooked peeled shrimp
pinch of cayenne pepper

1¼ cups Béchamel Sauce
(see page 12)
½ cup freshly grated
Parmesan cheese
2 large tomatoes, sliced
1 tsp dried oregano
salt and pepper

NUTRITIONAL INFORMATION

Calories	.478
Protein	.27g
Carbohydrate	.57g
Sugars	.6g
Fat	.17g
Saturates	.7g

variation

Cremini mushrooms would work very well in this recipe because they have a stronger flavor than white ones.

cook's tip

Fennel imparts a delicate aniseed flavor to dishes and goes very well with fish. To prepare the fennel bulbs, cut off the stalk and root end, then slice the bulbs lengthwise.

1 Preheat the oven to 350°F/180°C. Bring a large pan of lightly salted water to a boil. Add the pasta, return to a boil, and cook for 8–10 minutes, or until tender but still firm to the bite. Drain and return to the pan. Add 2 tablespoons of the butter to the pasta, cover, shake the pan and keep warm.

2 Melt the remaining butter in a separate pan. Add the fennel and cook for 3–4 minutes. Stir in the mushrooms and cook for an additional 2 minutes. Stir in the shrimp, then remove the pan from the heat.

3 Stir the cayenne pepper, and the shrimp mixture into the Béchamel Sauce.

4 Grease a large ovenproof dish, then pour the mixture into the dish and spread evenly. Sprinkle over the Parmesan cheese and arrange the tomato slices in a ring around the edge. Brush the tomatoes with olive oil, then sprinkle over the oregano. Bake in the oven for 25 minutes, or until golden brown. Serve immediately.

fillets of red snapper & pasta

serves 4   **prep: 15 mins** ⏲   **cook: 1 hr** ⏲

This simple recipe perfectly complements the sweet flavor and delicate texture of the fish.

INGREDIENTS

2 lb 4 oz/1 kg red snapper fillets

1½ cups dry white wine

4 shallots, finely chopped

1 garlic clove, crushed

3 tbsp finely chopped mixed fresh herbs

finely grated rind and juice of 1 lemon

pinch of freshly grated nutmeg

3 anchovy fillets, coarsely chopped

salt and pepper

2 tbsp heavy cream

1 tsp cornstarch

1 lb/450 g dried vermicelli

TO GARNISH

1 fresh mint sprig

lemon slices

lemon rind

NUTRITIONAL INFORMATION

Calories	.457
Protein	.39g
Carbohydrate	.44g
Sugars	.3g
Fat	.12g
Saturates	.5g

variation

You can substitute the dry white wine with the same amount of clear apple juice, if you prefer.

cook's tip

Use an unwaxed lemon, if possible, and wash before paring the rind. If only waxed lemons are available—or you are not sure—scrub with a vegetable brush.

1 Preheat the oven to 350°F/180°C. Place the red snapper fillets in a large casserole. Pour over the wine and add the shallots, garlic, herbs, lemon rind and juice, nutmeg, and anchovies. Season to taste with salt and pepper. Cover and bake in the preheated oven for 35 minutes.

2 Transfer the snapper to a warmed dish. Set aside and keep warm.

3 Pour the cooking liquid into a pan and bring to a boil. Simmer for 25 minutes, or until reduced by half. Mix the cream and cornstarch together, and stir into the sauce to thicken.

4 Meanwhile, bring a large, heavy-bottom pan of lightly salted water to a boil. Add the vermicelli, return to a boil, and cook for 8–10 minutes, or until tender but still firm to the bite. Drain the pasta and transfer to a warmed serving dish. Arrange the red snapper fillets on top of the vermicelli and pour over the sauce.

Garnish with a mint sprig, slices of lemon, and strips of lemon rind, and serve immediately.

tagliatelle with hake in chili sauce

serves 4   **prep: 10 mins** (ᒻ   **cook: 20 mins** (🕛

The surprisingly delicate flavor of this light, summery dish would make it a good choice for an alfresco lunch.

INGREDIENTS

bunch of fresh parsley

1 garlic clove, finely chopped

1 dried red chile, seeded

5 tbsp olive oil

1 lb/450 g hake fillets, skinned and cut into chunks

12 oz/350 g tomatoes, peeled, seeded, and diced

salt and pepper

12 oz/350 g dried tagliatelle

NUTRITIONAL INFORMATION	
Calories	.544
Protein	.32g
Carbohydrate	.68g
Sugars	.6g
Fat	.18g
Saturates	.2g

cook's tip

Make sure that you remove any fine bones remaining in the fish fillets. This is most easily done with tweezers.

1 Using a sharp knife, chop the parsley, garlic, and chile together. Heat half the olive oil in a large heavy-bottom skillet, add the herb mixture, and cook over low heat, stirring, for 1–2 minutes, or until the garlic gives off its aroma. Add the fish, cover, and cook for 5 minutes, then turn the fish and cook for an additional 5 minutes. Add the tomatoes and season to taste with salt and pepper. Re-cover the skillet and let simmer for an additional 5 minutes.

2 Meanwhile, bring a large heavy-bottom pan of lightly salted water to a boil. Add the pasta, return to a boil, and cook for 8–10 minutes, or until tender but still firm to the bite.

3 Drain the pasta, return to the pan, drizzle with the remaining olive oil, and toss. Transfer to a warmed serving platter and top with the fish mixture. Serve immediately.

fusilli with angler fish & broccoli

cook: 15 mins   **prep: 10 mins**   **serves 4**

This filling, clean-tasting dish is easy to make and takes so little time that it is ideal for a midweek family supper.

NUTRITIONAL INFORMATION	
Calories	.830
Protein	.32g
Carbohydrate	.77g
Sugars	.6g
Fat	.44g
Saturates	.22g

INGREDIENTS

4 oz/115 g broccoli, divided into florets

3 tbsp olive oil

12 oz/350 g angler fish fillet, skinned and cut into bite-size pieces

2 garlic cloves, crushed

salt and pepper

½ cup dry white wine

1 cup cream or panna da cucina

14 oz/400 g dried fusilli bucati

3 oz/85 g Gorgonzola cheese, diced

1 Divide the broccoli florets into tiny sprigs. Bring a pan of lightly salted water to a boil, add the broccoli, and cook for 2 minutes. Drain and refresh under cold running water.

2 Heat the olive oil in a large heavy-bottom skillet. Add the angler fish and garlic and season to taste with salt and pepper. Cook, stirring frequently, for 5 minutes, or until the fish is opaque. Pour in the white wine and cream and cook, stirring occasionally, for 5 minutes, or until the fish is cooked through and the sauce has thickened. Stir in the broccoli sprigs.

3 Meanwhile, bring a large heavy-bottom pan of lightly salted water to a boil. Add the pasta, return to a boil, and cook for 8–10 minutes, or until tender but still firm to the bite. Drain and tip the pasta into the pan with the fish, add the cheese, and toss lightly. Serve immediately.

variation

Substitute skinless, boneless chicken breasts for the angler fish and fusilli instead of fusilli bucati, if you prefer.

creamy smoked trout tagliatelle

serves 6   **prep: 15 mins** ⏲   **cook: 15 mins** ⏲

Contrasting colors and textures make this a good choice for family meals and for informal entertaining.

INGREDIENTS

2 carrots, cut into thin sticks	8 oz/225 g smoked trout fillets,
2 celery stalks, cut into thin sticks	skinned and cut into thin strips
1 zucchini, cut into thin sticks	⅞ cup cream cheese
1 leek, cut into thin sticks	⅔ cup dry white wine
1 cup peas	2 tbsp chopped fresh dill
⅔ cup Vegetable Stock	salt and pepper
(see page 12)	8 oz/225 g dried tagliatelle
	fresh dill sprigs, to garnish

NUTRITIONAL INFORMATION

Calories 370

Protein 16g

Carbohydrate 33g

Sugars 4g

Fat 19g

Saturates 10g

variation

You could use other smoked fish, such as buckling, halibut, or swordfish, instead of the smoked trout.

cook's tip

Dried pasta swells to nearly double its size when cooked, so it is best to use a large colander, preferably with a long handle, to drain it.

1 Place the carrots, celery, zucchini, leek, and peas into a large heavy-bottom pan and pour in the Vegetable Stock. Bring to a boil, reduce the heat, and let simmer for 5 minutes, or until tender and most of the stock has evaporated. Remove the pan from the heat, stir in the smoked trout, and cover to keep warm.

2 Place the cheese and wine in a separate large heavy-bottom pan and stir over low heat until the cheese has melted and the mixture is smooth. Stir in the chopped dill and season to taste with salt and pepper.

3 Meanwhile, bring a large heavy-bottom pan of lightly salted water to a boil.

Add the pasta, return to a boil, and cook for 8–10 minutes, or until tender but still firm to the bite. Drain and tip the pasta into the cheese sauce. Toss well to coat, then transfer to a warmed serving dish. Top with the smoked trout mixture, garnish with dill sprigs, and serve immediately.

shellfish bake

cook: 35 mins　　　**prep: 20 mins**　　　**serves 6**

variation

Substitute the conchiglie with other types of small pasta shapes, such as orechiette, if you prefer.

This lovely, light bake is a summertime treat and needs only a crisp salad and some crusty bread to make a filling meal.

INGREDIENTS

salt

12 oz/350 g dried conchiglie

3 oz/85 g butter, plus extra for greasing

2 fennel bulbs, thinly sliced and fronds set aside

6 oz/175 g mushrooms, thinly sliced

6 oz/175 g cooked shelled shrimp

6 oz/175 g crabmeat

pinch of cayenne pepper

1¼ cups Béchamel Sauce (see page 12)

½ cup freshly grated Parmesan cheese

2 beefsteak tomatoes, sliced

olive oil, for brushing

green salad, to serve

cook's tip

You can either use cooked fresh crabmeat or canned. If you wish to use fresh crab and time is limited, buy a ready-dressed crab from your fish merchant.

1 Preheat the oven to 350°F/180°C. Bring a large heavy-bottom pan of lightly salted water to a boil. Add the pasta, return to a boil, and cook for 8–10 minutes, or until tender but still firm to the bite. Drain well, return to the pan, and stir in 2 tablespoons of the butter. Cover and keep warm.

2 Meanwhile, melt the remaining butter in a large heavy-bottom skillet. Add the fennel and cook over medium heat for 5 minutes, or until softened. Stir in the mushrooms and cook for an additional 2 minutes. Stir in the shrimp and crabmeat, cook for an additional 1 minute, then remove the skillet from the heat.

3 Grease 6 small ovenproof dishes with butter. Stir the cayenne pepper into the Béchamel Sauce, add the shellfish mixture and pasta, then spoon into the prepared dishes. Sprinkle with the Parmesan cheese and arrange the tomato slices on top, then brush the tomatoes with a little olive oil.

4 Bake in the preheated oven for 25 minutes, or until golden brown. Serve hot with a green salad.

crab ravioli

serves 4   **prep: 30 mins, plus 1 hr resting**   **cook: 30 mins**

Spicy and succulent, crab-filled ravioli are sure to impress your guests for a meal celebrating a special occasion.

INGREDIENTS

6 scallions

12 oz/350 g crabmeat

2 tsp finely chopped fresh gingerroot

⅛–¼ tsp chili or Tabasco sauce

1 lb 9 oz/700 g tomatoes, peeled, seeded, and coarsely chopped

1 garlic clove, finely chopped

1 tbsp white wine vinegar

1 quantity Basic Pasta Dough (see page 13)

all-purpose flour, for dusting

salt

2 tbsp heavy cream or panna da cucina

shredded scallions, to garnish

NUTRITIONAL INFORMATION

Calories	450
Protein	29g
Carbohydrate	46g
Sugars	7g
Fat	19g
Saturates	7g

variation

For a change, use tomato, beet, or spinach-flavored pasta instead of the plain.

1 Thinly slice the scallions, keeping the white and green parts separate. Mix the green scallions, crabmeat, ginger, and chili sauce to taste together in a bowl. Cover with plastic wrap and let chill in the refrigerator until required.

2 Place the tomatoes in a food processor and process to a purée. Place the garlic, white scallions, and vinegar in a heavy-bottom pan and add the puréed tomatoes. Bring to a boil, stirring frequently, then reduce the heat and let simmer gently for 10 minutes. Remove from the heat and set aside.

3 Divide the Pasta Dough in half and roll out on a lightly floured counter. Make the ravioli (see page 101, Step 2), filling them with the crabmeat mixture. Place the ravioli on a dish towel and let rest for 1 hour.

4 Bring a large heavy-bottom pan of lightly salted water to a boil. Add the ravioli, in batches, return to a boil, and cook for 5 minutes. Remove with a slotted spoon and drain on paper towels. Meanwhile, gently heat the tomato sauce and whisk in the cream. Place the ravioli in a warmed serving dishes, pour the sauce over them, garnish with shredded scallions, and serve.

mussels & bucatini packages

cook: 25 mins   **prep: 15 mins**   **serves 4**

Dishes served in paper packages are always fun for family and friends and are a good way of ensuring that food is served hot.

NUTRITIONAL INFORMATION	
Calories	.500
Protein	.24g
Carbohydrate	.67g
Sugars	.4g
Fat	.14g
Saturates	.2g

INGREDIENTS

12 garlic cloves, lightly crushed, plus 1 garlic clove, finely chopped

2 lemons, sliced

2 lb 4 oz/1 kg live mussels, scrubbed and debearded (see Cook's Tip)

⅔ cup dry white wine

12 oz/350 g dried bucatini

4 tbsp olive oil

4 tbsp finely chopped fresh flatleaf parsley

salt and pepper

4 tbsp strained tomatoes

cook's tip

Before cooking, discard any mussels with broken shells or any that refuse to close when tapped. Use parchment paper rather than waxed paper for the packages, so that the mussels don't stick.

1 Preheat the oven to 350°F/180°C. Cut out 4 x 10-inch/25-cm squares of parchment paper. Place the crushed garlic, lemons, and mussels in a large heavy-bottom pan and pour in the wine. Cover tightly and cook over high heat, shaking the pan occasionally, for 5 minutes, or until the shells have opened. Remove the mussels with a slotted spoon and discard any that remain closed. Strain the cooking liquid through a cheesecloth-lined strainer and set aside. Remove the mussels from their shells and chop about one-third of them.

2 Bring a large heavy-bottom pan of lightly salted water to a boil. Add the pasta, return to a boil, and cook for 6–8 minutes, or until nearly tender.

3 Meanwhile, heat the oil in a large skillet. Add the garlic, parsley, and chopped mussels and cook, stirring, for 1 minute. Drain the pasta and add it to the skillet with the remaining mussels and 4 tablespoons of the strained cooking liquid. Season to taste with pepper and cook for 1 minute, then remove from the heat.

4 Divide the mixture between the paper squares. Top each portion with 1 tablespoon of strained tomatoes. Fold over the edges to seal, transfer to a baking sheet, and bake in the oven for 10 minutes. Serve.

mixed shellfish with angel hair pasta

serves 4 **prep: 20 mins** ⏲ **cook: 10 mins** ⏲

A stir-fried shellfish medley with a soy sauce dressing, served on a bed of fine pasta strands, is a kind of Westernized chow mein.

INGREDIENTS

3 oz/85 g prepared squid	12 oz/350 g capelli d'angelo
1 tsp cornstarch	3 tbsp peanut oil
1 tbsp water	2 oz/55 g snow peas
1 egg white	1 tbsp dark soy sauce
4 prepared scallops, sliced	1 tbsp dry sherry
3 oz/85 g raw shrimp, shelled	½ tsp light brown sugar
and deveined	2 scallions, shredded
salt	

NUTRITIONAL INFORMATION

Calories	.468
Protein	.26g
Carbohydrate	.70g
Sugars	.4g
Fat	.11g
Saturates	.2g

variation

Substitute the snow peas with the same amount of sugar snap peas and use corn oil instead of the peanut oil, if you prefer.

cook's tip

If you are using a wok, heat it first without any oil until hot, then add the oil and swirl it round to cover the bottom and sides of the wok. Preheating the wok beforehand prevents the food sticking.

1 Open out the squid and, with a sharp knife, score the inside with criss-cross lines. Cut into small pieces, about ¾-inch/2-cm square. Place in a bowl and cover with boiling water. When the squares have curled up, drain and rinse in cold water. Mix the cornstarch and water together in a small bowl until a smooth paste forms and stir in about half the egg white. Add the scallops and shrimp and toss until well coated.

2 Bring a large heavy-bottom pan of lightly salted water to a boil. Add the pasta, return to a boil, and cook for 5 minutes, or until tender but still firm to the bite.

3 Meanwhile, heat the oil in a preheated wok or heavy-bottom skillet. Add the snow peas, squid, scallops, and shrimp, and stir-fry for 2 minutes. Stir in the soy sauce, sherry, sugar, and scallions, and cook, stirring, for 1 minute. Drain the pasta and divide it between warmed plates. Top with the shellfish and serve immediately.

macaroni & tuna fish layer

serves 2   **prep: 20 mins**   **cook: 50 mins**

A layer of tuna fish with garlic, mushroom, and red bell pepper is sandwiched between two layers of macaroni with a crunchy topping.

INGREDIENTS

4½–5½ oz/125–150 g dried macaroni

1 tbsp olive oil

1 garlic clove, crushed

2 oz/55 g white mushrooms, sliced

½ red bell pepper, thinly sliced

7 oz/200 g canned tuna in spring water, drained and flaked

½ tsp dried oregano

salt and pepper

SAUCE

2 tbsp butter or margarine, plus extra for greasing

1 tbsp all-purpose flour

1 cup milk

2 tomatoes, sliced

2 tbsp dried bread crumbs

½ cup grated mature Cheddar or Parmesan cheese

NUTRITIONAL INFORMATION

Calories	.691
Protein	.41g
Carbohydrate	.62g
Sugars	.10g
Fat	.33g
Saturates	.15g

variation

Replace the tuna with chopped cooked chicken, beef, pork, or ham, or with 3–4 sliced hard-cooked eggs.

cook's tip

When cooking the macaroni, you can add 1 tablespoon of oil to the water to help prevent the pasta sticking, although it is not necessary if you use a large pan. Keep the water at a rolling boil.

1 Preheat the oven to 400°F/200°C. Bring a large pan of lightly salted water to a boil. Add the macaroni, return to a boil, and cook for 10–12 minutes, or until tender but still firm to the bite. Drain, rinse, and drain thoroughly.

2 Heat the olive oil in a skillet and cook the garlic, mushrooms, and bell pepper until soft. Add the tuna, oregano, and add salt and pepper to taste. Heat through. Grease a 4-cup/1-liter ovenproof dish with a little butter or margarine. Add half of the cooked macaroni, cover with the tuna mixture, then add the remaining macaroni.

3 To make the sauce, melt the butter or margarine in a pan, stir in the flour and cook for 1 minute. Add the milk gradually and bring to a boil. Simmer for 1–2 minutes, stirring constantly, until thickened. Season to taste with salt and pepper. Pour the sauce over the macaroni. Lay the sliced tomatoes over the

sauce and sprinkle with the bread crumbs and cheese. Cook in the preheated oven for 25 minutes, or until piping hot and the top is well browned.

shellfish & pasta packages

serves 4 | **prep: 15 mins** | **cook: 30 mins**

What more quintessentially Italian combination could there be than spaghetti, mussels, shrimp, and tomatoes?

INGREDIENTS

1 lemon, sliced

1 lb/450 g live mussels, scrubbed and debearded (see Cook's Tip)

½ cup dry white wine

1 tbsp olive oil

2 garlic cloves, finely chopped

1 lb/450 g tomatoes, peeled

8 oz/225 g cooked shelled shrimp

2 tbsp chopped fresh parsley

salt and pepper

12 oz/350 g dried spaghetti

fresh flatleaf parsley sprigs and lemon halves, to garnish

NUTRITIONAL INFORMATION

Calories	.430
Protein	.30g
Carbohydrate	.69g
Sugars	.7g
Fat	.4g
Saturates	.1g

cook's tip

Before cooking, discard any mussels with damaged or broken shells or any that refuse to close when sharply tapped with a knife.

1 Preheat the oven to 300°F/150°C. Cut out 4 rectangles of parchment paper, 12 x 18 inches/30 x 46 cm. Place the sliced lemon and mussels in a large heavy-bottom pan and add the wine. Cover and cook over high heat, shaking the pan occasionally, for 5 minutes, or until the shells have opened. Remove the mussels with a slotted spoon, reserving the cooking liquid. Discard any that remain closed. Strain the liquid through a cheesecloth-lined strainer and set aside.

2 Heat the olive oil in a skillet, add the garlic and cook for 1 minute. Chop the tomatoes, then add to the skillet and cook over medium heat for 10 minutes, or until softened. Stir in the reserved cooking liquid. Reduce the heat, add the shrimp and parsley, and let simmer for 2 minutes. Season to taste with salt and pepper.

3 Meanwhile, bring a large heavy-bottom pan of lightly salted water to a boil. Add the pasta, return to a boil, and cook for 8–10 minutes, or until tender but still firm to the bite. Drain and tip into a bowl. Add the tomato mixture and toss well. Stir in the mussels. Divide the mixture between the paper rectangles and fold over the edges to seal. Transfer to a baking sheet and cook in the oven for 10 minutes. Open up the packages and garnish with the parsley. Serve.

fettuccine with saffron mussels

⏱ **cook: 20 mins**   ⏱ **prep: 15 mins**   **serves 4**

A classic combination and a sophisticated pasta dish,
this looks mouthwatering and tastes superb.

NUTRITIONAL INFORMATION	
Calories	.510
Protein	.29g
Carbohydrate	.76g
Sugars	.6g
Fat	.9g
Saturates	.3g

INGREDIENTS

pinch of saffron threads

¾ cup hot water

2 lb 4 oz/1 kg live mussels, scrubbed
and debearded (see Cook's Tip)

½ cup cold water

1 tbsp corn oil

1 small onion, finely chopped

2 tbsp all-purpose flour

½ cup dry white vermouth

4 tbsp freshly grated Parmesan cheese

2 tbsp chopped chives, plus extra
to garnish

salt and pepper

12 oz/350 g dried fettuccine

cook's tip

Use saffron threads rather than ground saffron, as the powder may have been adulterated. Before cooking, discard any mussels with broken shells or any that refuse to close when tapped with a knife.

1 Place the saffron in a small bowl, add the hot water, and let soak. Place the mussels in a large heavy-bottom pan. Add the cold water, cover, and cook over high heat, shaking the pan occasionally, for 5 minutes, or until the shells have opened. Remove the mussels with a slotted spoon, reserving the liquid. Discard any that have not opened and remove the remainder from their shells. Strain the cooking liquid through a cheesecloth-lined strainer and set aside.

2 Heat the oil in a skillet. Add the onion and cook over low heat, stirring, for 5 minutes, or until softened. Sprinkle in the flour and cook, stirring, for 1 minute. Remove from the heat. Mix the vermouth and saffron liquid together and gradually whisk in to the skillet. Return to the heat and let simmer, stirring, for 2–3 minutes, or until thickened. Stir in 4 tablespoons of the reserved cooking liquid, the cheese, mussels, and chives, and season with salt and pepper. Let simmer for 4 minutes, or until hot.

3 Meanwhile, bring a large heavy-bottom pan of lightly salted water to a boil. Add the pasta, return to a boil, and cook for 8–10 minutes, or until tender but still firm to the bite. Drain and transfer to a large, warmed serving dish. Add the mussels and sauce, toss well, garnish with extra chopped chives, and serve.

linguine with clams in tomato sauce

🕐 **cook: 35 mins**   🕐 **prep: 20 mins**   **serves 4**

variation

Substitute the parsley with the same amount of shredded basil, and if you prefer a less spicy sauce, omit the chile in Step 2.

Pasta eaters argue passionately about the right way to serve clams with pasta. Some are adherents to the classic Spaghetti con Vongole (see page 162) and are horrified by the combination with tomatoes and cheese, while others love this typically Neapolitan recipe. Actually, both are wonderful.

INGREDIENTS

1 cup dry white wine

2 garlic cloves, coarsely chopped

4 tbsp fresh flatleaf parsley, coarsely chopped

2 lb 4 oz/1 kg live clams, scrubbed

2 tbsp olive oil

1 onion, chopped

8 plum tomatoes, peeled, seeded, and chopped

1 fresh red chile, seeded and chopped

salt and pepper

12 oz/350 g dried linguine

cook's tip

Before cooking, discard any clams with damaged or broken shells and any that refuse to close when sharply tapped with a knife.

1 Pour the wine into a large heavy-bottom pan and add the garlic, half the parsley, and the clams. Cover and cook over high heat, shaking the pan occasionally, for 5 minutes, or until the shells have opened. Remove the clams with a slotted spoon, reserving the cooking liquid. Discard any that have not opened and remove half of the remainder from their shells. Keep the shelled and unshelled clams in separate covered bowls. Strain the cooking liquid through a cheesecloth-lined strainer and set aside.

2 Heat the olive oil in a heavy-bottom pan. Add the onion and cook over low heat for 5 minutes, or until softened. Add the tomatoes, chile, and reserved cooking liquid, and season to taste with salt and pepper. Bring to a boil, partially cover, and let simmer for 20 minutes.

3 Meanwhile, bring a large heavy-bottom pan of lightly salted water to a boil. Add the pasta, return to a boil, and cook for 8–10 minutes, or until tender but still firm to the bite. Drain and transfer to a warmed serving dish.

4 Stir the shelled clams into the tomato sauce and heat through gently for 2–3 minutes. Pour over the pasta and toss. Garnish with the clams in their shells and remaining parsley. Serve.

spaghetti con vongole

serves 4   **prep: 15 mins**   **cook: 15 mins**

*This is the purist's classic combination of clams and pasta,
cooked simply in white wine and flavored with fresh parsley.*

INGREDIENTS

2 lb 4 oz/1 kg live clams, scrubbed

¾ cup water

¾ cup dry white wine

12 oz/350 g dried spaghetti

5 tbsp olive oil

2 garlic cloves, finely chopped

4 tbsp chopped fresh
flatleaf parsley

salt and pepper

NUTRITIONAL INFORMATION

Calories 512

Protein 23g

Carbohydrate 67g

Sugars 3g

Fat 16g

Saturates 2g

variation

If fresh clams are not available,
use 2 x 14 oz/400 g jars of clams.
Drain and rinse before adding to the
skillet in Step 3.

cook's tip

Shellfish, such as mussels and
clams, are always sold alive.
To test if they are alive, tap the
shell gently and if it closes
immediately, then it is alive.
If not, it is dead, and should
not be cooked or eaten.

1 Place the clams in a
large heavy-bottom
pan. Add the water and wine,
then cover and cook over high
heat, shaking the pan
occasionally, for 5 minutes, or
until the shells have opened.
Remove the clams with a
slotted spoon and strain the
liquid through a cheesecloth-
lined strainer into a small pan.
Bring to a boil and cook until

reduced by about half. Discard
any clams that have not
opened and remove the
remainder from their shells.

2 Bring a large heavy-
bottom pan of lightly
salted water to a boil. Add the
pasta, return to a boil, and
cook for 8–10 minutes, or until
tender but still firm to the bite.

3 Meanwhile, heat the
olive oil in a large
heavy-bottom skillet. Add the
garlic and cook, stirring
frequently, for 2 minutes. Add
the parsley and the reduced
cooking liquid and let simmer
gently. Drain the pasta and
add it to the skillet with the
clams. Season to taste with
salt and pepper and cook,
stirring constantly, for

4 minutes, or until the pasta
is coated and the clams have
heated through. Transfer to
a warmed serving dish and
serve immediately.

pasta omelet with shrimp

cook: 20 mins   **prep: 15 mins**   **serves 4**

NUTRITIONAL INFORMATION

Calories	.580
Protein	.33g
Carbohydrate	.65g
Sugars	.4g
Fat	.25g
Saturates	.7g

variation

Substitute the dried spaghetti with dried vermicelli or bucatini and replace the romano cheese with the same amount of Parmesan cheese.

This different approach to serving pasta provides an easy, nourishing midweek family supper with very little to clear up afterwards. A salad of mixed greens is the perfect complement.

INGREDIENTS

12 oz/350 g dried spaghetti

3 eggs

3 tbsp finely chopped fresh parsley

¾ cup freshly grated romano cheese

8 oz/225 g cooked shelled shrimp, deveined

salt and pepper

4 tbsp olive oil

whole cooked shrimp, to garnish

mixed salad greens, to serve

cook's tip

To speed up the cooking process, gently stir the egg and pasta mixture from the edge of the skillet into the center once the base has lightly set.

1 Bring a large heavy-bottom pan of lightly salted water to a boil. Add the pasta, return to a boil, and cook for 8–10 minutes, or until tender but still firm to the bite. Drain well, then rinse under cold running water and drain again. Set aside until required.

2 Beat the eggs with the parsley and cheese, then stir in the shrimp. Season to taste with salt and pepper and stir in the pasta.

3 Heat half the olive oil in a heavy-bottom skillet. Pour in the egg and pasta mixture, tilt the skillet to

spread it evenly and cook over medium heat, shaking the skillet occasionally, until the top of the omelet is starting to set and the underside is golden. Place a plate over the skillet and invert the two. Heat the remaining oil in the skillet, then slide the omelet back into the skillet to cook the

other side. Cut the omelet into wedges and transfer to warmed serving plates. Garnish with a few whole shrimp and serve immediately with mixed salad greens.

shrimp, peas & pasta

serves 4   **prep: 15 mins**   **cook: 20 mins**

This pretty pink and green dish would be a good choice for a summery supper, served with a glass of chilled white wine.

INGREDIENTS

pinch of saffron threads

1 cup dry white wine

3 tbsp olive oil

2 tbsp unsalted butter

1 shallot, chopped

2 cups peas

12 oz/350 g cooked shelled shrimp

12 oz/350 g dried fusilli bucati or ditali

salt and pepper

2 tbsp chopped fresh dill, to garnish

NUTRITIONAL INFORMATION	
Calories	590
Protein	34g
Carbohydrate	71g
Sugars	5g
Fat	17g
Saturates	5g

cook's tip

If you are using frozen cooked shrimp and/or frozen peas, make sure that they are thoroughly thawed before you start cooking this recipe.

1 Place the saffron in a small bowl, add the wine, and let soak. Heat the olive oil and butter in a large heavy-bottom skillet. Add the shallot and cook over low heat, stirring occasionally, for 5 minutes, or until softened. Add the peas and cooked shrimp and cook, stirring occasionally, for 2–3 minutes.

2 Bring a large heavy-bottom pan of lightly salted water to a boil. Add the pasta, return to a boil, and cook for 8–10 minutes, or until tender but still firm to the bite.

3 Meanwhile, stir the saffron and wine mixture into the skillet. Increase the heat and cook until the liquid is reduced by about half. Season to taste with salt and pepper. Drain the pasta and add to the skillet. Cook for 1–2 minutes, or until it is well coated with the sauce. Transfer to a warmed serving dish, sprinkle with dill, and serve.

spaghetti with shrimp & caviar

cook: 12 mins   **prep: 10 mins**   **serves 4**

Expensive and wonderfully over the top, this sophisticated dish with the luxurious taste of caviar is strictly for adults.

NUTRITIONAL INFORMATION

Calories	.720
Protein	.27g
Carbohydrate	.66g
Sugars	.4g
Fat	.33g
Saturates	.13g

INGREDIENTS

12 oz/350 g dried spaghetti

4 tbsp olive oil

3 scallions, thinly sliced

1 garlic clove, finely chopped

8 oz/225 g cooked shelled shrimp,

deveined, tails left on

½ cup lemon-flavored vodka

⅔ cup heavy cream or panna da cucina

8 tbsp caviar, plus extra to garnish

salt and pepper

fresh chives, to garnish

cook's tip

Genuine caviar is expensive and, as the sturgeon from which it comes is quite rare, prices are climbing. Pressed caviar, made from damaged eggs, is cheaper.

1 Bring a large heavy-bottom pan of lightly salted water to a boil. Add the pasta, return to a boil, and cook for 8–10 minutes, or until tender but still firm to the bite.

2 Meanwhile, heat the olive oil in a heavy-bottom skillet. Add the scallions and the garlic and cook over low heat, stirring occasionally, for 3–4 minutes, or until softened. Add the shrimp and cook, stirring occasionally, for 2 minutes. Pour in the vodka and cream and let simmer gently for 5 minutes. Remove the skillet from the heat. With a slotted spoon, remove the shrimp from the sauce and set aside.

3 Stir the caviar into the cream sauce and season to taste with salt and pepper. Drain the pasta and tip it into the sauce. Toss to coat and transfer to warmed serving plates. Garnish with the shrimp, extra caviar, and chives, and serve immediately.

linguine with shrimp & scallops

serves 6   **prep: 15 mins** ⏾   **cook: 30 mins** ⏱

Using the shrimp shells to flavor the sauce—they are discarded before serving—gives a subtle depth to this fabulous dish.

INGREDIENTS

1 lb/450 g raw shrimp

2 tbsp butter

2 shallots, finely chopped

1 cup dry white vermouth

1½ cups water

1 lb/450 g dried linguine

2 tbsp olive oil

1 lb/450 g prepared scallops, thawed if frozen

2 tbsp chopped fresh chives

salt and pepper

NUTRITIONAL INFORMATION

Calories 487

Protein 33g

Carbohydrate 61g

Sugars 5g

Fat 10g

Saturates 3g

---

variation

Substitute the spaghetti with linguine and if chives are unavailable, then use spring onion tops.

cook's tip

Both scallops and shrimp become tough when over-cooked, so keep stirring and do not cook for longer than necessary in Step 3.

1 Shell and devein the shrimp, reserving the shells. Melt the butter in a heavy-bottom skillet. Add the shallots and cook over low heat, stirring occasionally, for 5 minutes, or until softened. Add the shrimp shells and cook, stirring constantly, for 1 minute. Pour in the vermouth and cook, stirring, for 1 minute. Add the water, bring to a boil,

then reduce the heat and let simmer for 10 minutes, or until the liquid has reduced by half. Remove the skillet from the heat.

2 Bring a large heavy-bottom pan of lightly salted water to a boil. Add the pasta, return to a boil, and cook for 8–10 minutes, or until tender but still firm to the bite.

3 Meanwhile, heat the oil in a separate heavy-bottom skillet. Add the scallops and shrimp and cook, stirring frequently, for 2 minutes, or until the scallops are opaque and the shrimp have changed color. Strain the shrimp-shell stock into the skillet. Drain the pasta and add to the skillet with the chives and season to taste

with salt and pepper. Toss well over low heat for 1 minute, then serve. .

scallops with black tagliatelle

serves 4   **prep: 15 mins**   **cook: 12–15 mins**

Serving this dramatic looking dish is sure to impress your guests—nor will they be disappointed when they taste it.

INGREDIENTS

12 oz/350 g prepared scallops, thawed if frozen

3 tbsp olive oil

1 onion, finely chopped

1 garlic clove, finely chopped

2 carrots, cut into thin sticks

12 oz/350 g black tagliatelle

2 tbsp dry white wine

2 tbsp anise, such as Pernod

1 tbsp chopped fresh dill

⅔ cup heavy cream or panna da cucina

salt and pepper

NUTRITIONAL INFORMATION	
Calories	.690
Protein	.32g
Carbohydrate	.75g
Sugars	.9g
Fat	.29g
Saturates	.13g

variation

If you are unable to find black tagliatelle, then use plain or even spinach-flavored tagliatelle instead.

cook's tip

To prepare a scallop, hold the shell flat-side up, insert a knife blade to cut the top muscle, then separate the shells. Slide the blade under the "skirt" to cut the lower muscle. Remove the white muscle and coral.

1 Separate the corals from the scallops, if necessary, and cut the white muscle in half. Heat the olive oil in a skillet. Add the onion, garlic, and carrots and cook over low heat for 8 minutes, or until softened.

2 Meanwhile, bring a large heavy-bottom pan of lightly salted water to a boil.

Add the pasta, return to a boil, and cook for 8–10 minutes, or until tender but still firm to the bite.

3 Add the scallops with any corals, wine, anise, and dill to the skillet. Cover and let simmer for 1 minute. With a slotted spoon, transfer the scallops, corals, and vegetables to a large heatproof plate, then

cover and keep warm. Bring the cooking juices to a boil and cook until reduced by about half, then stir in the cream.

4 Return the scallops, corals, and vegetables to the skillet, season to taste with salt and pepper, and heat through gently. Drain the pasta and transfer to a warmed serving dish. Pour the scallops

and their sauce over the pasta, toss well, and serve immediately.

cavatappi with squid in fennel sauce

serves 4　　　　　**prep: 15 mins** ⌫　　　　　**cook: 30 mins** ⏲

A delicious combination of squid and fennel is perfect for any special occasion. Serve with mixed salad greens and crusty bread.

INGREDIENTS

1 tbsp olive oil

12 oz/350 g prepared squid, sliced into rings (see Cook's Tip)

4 tbsp anise, such as Pernod

14 oz/400 g canned chopped tomatoes

1 fennel bulb, grated

2 shallots, finely chopped

12 oz/350 g dried cavatappi

salt and pepper

NUTRITIONAL INFORMATION

Calories	.446
Protein	.25g
Carbohydrate	.70g
Sugars	.7g
Fat	.5g
Saturates	.1g

1 Heat the olive oil in a heavy-bottom skillet. Add the squid and cook, stirring frequently, for 2 minutes. Add the anise and cook for 1 minute, then transfer the squid to a plate with a slotted spoon. Add the tomatoes, fennel, and shallots to the skillet, cover, and let simmer, stirring occasionally, for 20 minutes, or until thickened.

2 Meanwhile, bring a large heavy-bottom pan of lightly salted water to a boil. Add the pasta, return to a boil, and cook for 8–10 minutes, or until tender but still firm to the bite.

3 Return the squid to the skillet, season to taste with salt and pepper, and heat through gently for

2 minutes. Drain the pasta and transfer to a warmed bowl. Spoon the squid sauce over the pasta, toss well, and serve immediately.

cook's tip

To prepare squid, pull the head from the body. Cut off the tentacles and squeeze out the beak. Remove and discard the "quill" from the body sac. Rinse the sac under cold running water and rub off the skin.

penne with squid & tomatoes

⏲ **cook: 25 mins**   ⏱ **prep: 15 mins**   **serves 4**

All the ingredients, including the pasta, cook together in a single pan for an easy dish and a delicious melding of flavors.

NUTRITIONAL INFORMATION

Calories	.485
Protein	.23g
Carbohydrate	.53g
Sugars	.11g
Fat	.19g
Saturates	.2g

INGREDIENTS

8 oz/225 g dried penne

12 oz/350 g prepared squid
(see Cook's Tip, page 172)

6 tbsp olive oil

2 onions, sliced

1 cup Fish or Chicken Stock
(see page 12)

⅔ cup full-bodied red wine

14 oz/400 g canned chopped tomatoes

2 tbsp tomato paste

1 tbsp chopped fresh marjoram

1 bay leaf

salt and pepper

2 tbsp chopped fresh parsley

cook's tip

The sauce should be quite thick. If it seems too liquid by the time the pasta is tender, boil vigorously for a couple of minutes to reduce.

1 Bring a large heavy-bottom pan of lightly salted water to a boil. Add the pasta, return to a boil, and cook for 3 minutes, then drain and set aside until required. With a sharp knife, cut the squid into strips.

2 Heat the olive oil in a large flameproof dish or casserole. Add the onions and cook over low heat, stirring occasionally, for 5 minutes, or until softened. Add the squid and Fish Stock, bring to a boil, and let simmer for 3 minutes. Stir in the wine, chopped tomatoes and their can juices, tomato paste, marjoram, and bay leaf. Season to taste with salt and pepper. Bring to a boil and cook for 5 minutes, or until slightly reduced.

3 Add the pasta, return to a boil, and let simmer for 5–7 minutes, or until tender but still firm to the bite. Remove and discard the bay leaf, stir in the parsley, and serve immediately, straight from the dish.

macaroni & squid casserole

serves 6　　　　　**prep: 15 mins** ↻　　　　　**cook: 35 mins** ⏲

This pasta dish is quick and easy to make and is a very hearty meal for a large number of guests. Serve with crusty bread, if you like.

INGREDIENTS

8 oz/225 g dried short-cut macaroni

2 tbsp chopped fresh parsley

salt and pepper

SAUCE

12 oz/350 g cleaned squid, cut into ½-inch/4-cm strips

6 tbsp olive oil

2 onions, sliced

1 cup Fish Stock (see page 12)

⅔ cup red wine

12 oz/350 g tomatoes, peeled and thinly sliced

2 tbsp tomato paste

1 tsp dried oregano

2 bay leaves

variation

You can use other short pasta shapes, such as farfalle, fusilli, and penne, if you prefer.

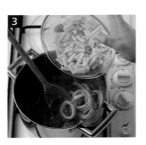

cook's tip

To peel tomatoes, mark a cross in the skin with a knife, then place in a bowl and pour over enough boiling water to cover. Leave for 20 seconds, then drain and rinse. Peel off the skin starting at the cross.

1　Bring a large, heavy-bottom pan of lightly salted water to a boil. Add the macaroni, return to a boil, and cook for only 3 minutes. Drain in a colander, return to the pan, cover, and keep warm.

2　To make the sauce, heat the olive oil in a pan and cook the onion until translucent. Add the squid

and stock and simmer for 5 minutes. Pour on the wine and add the tomatoes, tomato paste, oregano, and bay leaves. Bring to a boil, season with salt and pepper, and cook for 5 minutes.

3　Add the pasta, stir well, cover the pan and continue simmering for 10 minutes, or until the

macaroni and squid are almost tender. By this time the sauce should be thick and syrupy. If it is too liquid, uncover the pan and continue cooking for a few minutes. Taste the sauce and adjust the seasoning, if necessary.

4　Remove the bay leaves and stir in most of the parsley, reserving a little to

garnish. Transfer to a large warmed serving dish. Sprinkle on the remaining parsley and serve hot.

spaghetti & shellfish

serves 4 | **prep: 35 mins** | **cook: 30 mins**

*Frozen shelled shrimp from the freezer can become the star
ingredient in this colorful and tasty dish.*

INGREDIENTS

8 oz/225 g dried short-cut spaghetti,
or long spaghetti broken into
6-inch/15-cm lengths

1 tbsp olive oil

1¼ cups Chicken Stock
(see page 12)

1 tsp lemon juice

1 small cauliflower, cut into florets

2 carrots, sliced thinly

4½ oz/125 g snow peas

2 oz/55 g butter

1 onion, sliced

8 oz/225 g zucchini, thinly sliced

1 garlic clove, chopped

12 oz/350 g frozen peeled
shrimp, thawed

salt and pepper

2 tbsp chopped fresh parsley

¼ cup freshly grated
Parmesan cheese

½ tsp paprika, to sprinkle

4 unpeeled shrimp, to garnish
(optional)

crusty bread, to serve

NUTRITIONAL INFORMATION

Calories	.510
Protein	.33g
Carbohydrate	.44g
Sugars	.38g
Fat	.24g
Saturates	.11g

variation

Use broccoli instead of the cauliflower,
and sugar snap peas instead of the
snow peas, if you prefer.

cook's tip

To prepare snow peas, either
cut the stalk off with a knife
or snap it off with your fingers
and pull off the string. This
preparation also applies to
sugar snap peas.

1 Bring a large, heavy-
bottom pan of lightly
salted water to a boil. Add
the spaghetti, return to
the boil and cook for
8–10 minutes, or until tender
but still firm to the bite. Drain,
then return to the pan and stir
in the olive oil. Cover and
keep warm.

2 Bring the Chicken Stock
and lemon juice to a
boil. Add the cauliflower
and carrots and cook for
3–4 minutes, until they are
barely tender. Remove with a
slotted spoon and set aside.
Add the snow peas and cook
for 1–2 minutes, until they start
to soften. Remove and add to
the other vegetables. Reserve
the stock for future use.

3 Melt half of the butter
in a skillet over
medium heat and cook the
onion and zucchini for
3 minutes. Add the garlic
and shrimp and cook for an
additional 2–3 minutes, until
thoroughly heated through.

4 Stir in the reserved
vegetables and heat
through. Season to taste with

salt and pepper, then stir in the
remaining butter. Transfer the
spaghetti to a warmed serving
dish. Pour on the sauce and
parsley. Toss well using 2 forks,
until thoroughly coated.
Sprinkle on the grated cheese
and paprika, and garnish with
upeeled shrimp, if using.
Serve immediately.

fish & vegetable lasagna

serves 6   **prep: 25 mins** ⏲   **cook: 50 mins** ⏲

Layers of cheese sauce, smoked cod and whole wheat lasagna can be assembled overnight and left ready to cook on the following day.

INGREDIENTS

8 sheets dried whole-wheat lasagna

1 lb 2 oz/500 g smoked cod

2½ cups milk

1 tbsp lemon juice

8 peppercorns

2 bay leaves

few fresh parsley stalks

½ cup freshly grated mature Cheddar cheese

¼ cup freshly grated Parmesan cheese

salt and pepper

few whole shrimp, to garnish

SAUCE

2 oz/55 g butter, plus extra for greasing

1 large onion, sliced

1 green bell pepper, cored, seeded, and chopped

1 small zucchini, sliced

scant ½ cup all-purpose plain flour

⅔ cup white wine

⅔ cup light cream

4½ oz/125 g shelled shrimp

½ cup freshly grated mature Cheddar cheese

variation

Replace the red bell pepper with a green one and use spinach-flavored lasagna sheets instead of whole-wheat.

cook's tip

If your time is limited, then use dried no-precook lasagna sheets. These are available from most large supermarkets and Italian delicatessens.

1 Preheat the oven to 375°F/190°C. Bring a large pan of lightly salted water to a boil. Add the lasagna and cook according to the package instructions, until almost tender. Drain and set aside.

2 Place the smoked cod, milk, lemon juice, peppercorns, bay leaves, and parsley in a skillet. Bring to a boil, cover, and simmer for 10 minutes. Lift the fish from the skillet. Remove the skin and bones. Flake the fish. Strain and reserve the liquor.

3 To make the sauce, melt the butter in a skillet and cook the onion, bell pepper, and zucchini for 2–3 minutes. Stir in the flour and cook for 1 minute. Gradually add the fish liquor, then stir in the wine, cream and shrimp. Simmer for 2 minutes. Remove from the heat, add the cheese, and season to taste with salt and pepper.

4 Grease a shallow baking dish. Pour in a quarter of the sauce and spread evenly over the base. Cover the sauce with 3 sheets of lasagna, then with a quarter of the sauce. Arrange the fish on top, then cover with half of the remaining sauce. Finish with the remaining lasagna, then the rest of the sauce. Sprinkle the Cheddar and Parmesan cheeses over the top. Bake for 25 minutes, or until golden brown and bubbling. Garnish with shrimp and serve.

farfallini buttered lobster

serves 4   **prep: 30 mins** ⟳   **cook: 25 mins** ⟳

*This is one of those dishes that looks almost too lovely to eat—
but you should! Perfect for entertaining family and friends.*

INGREDIENTS

2 lobsters (about 1 lb 9 oz/700 g each),
split into halves

juice and grated rind of 1 lemon

4 oz/115 g butter

4 tbsp fresh white bread crumbs

2 tbsp brandy

5 tbsp heavy cream

1 lb/450 g dried farfallini

salt and pepper

½ cup freshly grated
Parmesan cheese

TO GARNISH

1 lemon, sliced

1 kiwi fruit, sliced

4 unshelled cooked jumbo shrimp

fresh dill sprigs

NUTRITIONAL INFORMATION

Calories	.686
Protein	.45g
Carbohydrate	.44g
Sugars	.1g
Fat	.36g
Saturates	.19g

variation

Substitute the brandy for the same amount of whiskey, if you prefer, and use other dried pasta shapes if farfallini is unavailable.

cook's tip

Before filling the lobster shells with the mixture, make sure that they are completely dried out, otherwise the finished dish may become soggy.

1 Preheat the oven to 325°F/160°C. Discard the stomach sac, vein, and gills from each lobster. Remove the meat from the tail and chop. Crack the claws and legs, remove the meat and chop. Transfer the meat to a bowl and add the lemon juice and lemon rind. Clean the shells and place in the warm oven to dry out.

2 Melt 2 tablespoons of the butter in a skillet. Add the bread crumbs and cook for 3 minutes, until crisp and golden brown. Melt the remaining butter in a separate pan. Add the lobster meat and heat through gently. Add the brandy and cook for an additional 3 minutes, then add the cream and season to taste with salt and pepper.

3 Meanwhile, bring a large pan of lightly salted water to a boil. Add the farfallini and cook for 8–10 minutes, or until tender but still firm to the bite. Drain and spoon the pasta into the clean lobster shells.

4 Preheat the broiler to medium. Top with the buttered lobster and sprinkle

with a little Parmesan cheese and the bread crumbs. Broil for 2–3 minutes, or until golden brown. Transfer the lobster shells to a warmed serving dish, garnish with the lemon slices, kiwi fruit, jumbo shrimp, and dill sprigs, and serve immediately.

pasta & shrimp packages

serves 4   **prep: 15 mins** 🕐   **cook: 30 mins** 🕐

This is the ideal dish when you have guests because the packages can be prepared in advance, then cooked when ready to eat.

INGREDIENTS

1 lb/450 g dried fettuccine

⅔ cup store-bought pesto

4 tsp extra virgin olive oil

1 lb 10 oz/750 g large raw shrimp,
shelled and deveined

2 garlic cloves, crushed

½ cup dry white wine

salt and pepper

NUTRITIONAL INFORMATION

Calories 640

Protein 50g

Carbohydrate 42g

Sugars 1g

Fat 29g

Saturates 4g

cook's tip

Be very careful when unwrapping the packages because they will be extremely hot. Let your guests unwrap them at the dinner table.

1 Preheat the oven to 400°F/200°C. Cut out 4 x 12-inch/30-cm squares of waxed paper. Bring a large, heavy-bottom pan of lightly salted water to a boil. Add the fettuccine, return to a boil, and cook for 2–3 minutes, or until just softened. Drain and set aside until required.

2 Mix the fettuccine and half of the pesto together in a bowl. Spread out the paper squares and place 1 teaspoon of olive oil in the center of each. Divide the fettuccine between the squares, then divide the shrimp and place on top of the fettuccine. Mix the remaining pesto and the garlic together and spoon it over the shrimp. Season each

package and sprinkle with the white wine. Dampen the edges of the waxed paper and wrap the packages loosely, twisting the edges to seal.

3 Place the packages on a cookie sheet and bake in the preheated oven for 10–15 minutes. Transfer the packages to plates and serve.

pasta shells with mussels

⏱ cook: 25 mins   ⏱ prep: 15 mins   serves 6

Serve this delicious aromatic seafood dish to family and friends who admit to a love of garlic. Serve with plenty of warm crusty bread.

NUTRITIONAL INFORMATION

Calories 686

Protein 30g

Carbohydrate 36g

Sugars 2g

Fat 45g

Saturates 27g

INGREDIENTS

2 lb 12 oz/1.25 kg live mussels, cleaned (see cook's tip)

1 cup dry white wine

2 large onions, chopped

4 oz/115 g unsalted butter

6 large garlic cloves, finely chopped

5 tbsp chopped fresh parsley

1¼ cups heavy cream

14 oz/400 g dried pasta shells

salt and pepper

crusty bread, to serve

cook's tip

To clean the mussels, scrub them under cold running water and pull off any beards that are still attached to them. Discard any mussels that do not close immediately when sharply tapped with a knife.

1 Place the mussels in a large, heavy-bottom pan, together with the wine and half of the onions. Cover and cook over a medium heat, shaking the pan frequently, for 2–3 minutes, or until the shells open. Remove the pan from the heat. Strain the mussels and reserve the cooking liquid. Discard any mussels that have not opened. Strain the cooking liquid through a clean cloth into a glass pitcher or bowl and set aside.

2 Melt the butter in a pan. Add the remaining onion and cook until translucent. Stir in the garlic and cook for 1 minute. Gradually stir in the reserved cooking liquid. Stir in the parsley and cream, and season to taste with salt and pepper. Bring to simmering point over low heat.

3 Meanwhile, bring a large pan of lightly salted water to a boil. Add the pasta, and cook for 8–10 minutes, or until tender, but still firm to the bite. Drain, and keep warm.

4 Set aside a few mussels for the garnish and remove the remainder from their shells. Stir the shelled mussels into the cream sauce and warm briefly. Transfer the pasta to a serving dish. Pour over the sauce and toss to coat. Garnish with the reserved mussels and serve.

salmon lasagna rolls

serves 4   **prep: 20 mins** ⏲   **cook: 35 mins** ⏲

Sheets of green lasagna are filled with a mixture of fresh salmon and oyster mushrooms. This recipe has been adapted for cooking in the microwave.

INGREDIENTS

8 sheets dried green lasagna

1 onion, sliced

1 tbsp butter, plus extra for greasing

½ red bell pepper, chopped

1 zucchini, diced

1 tsp chopped fresh gingerroot

4½ oz/125 g oyster mushrooms, preferably yellow, coarsely chopped

8 oz/225 g fresh salmon fillet, skinned, and cut into chunks

2 tbsp dry sherry

2 tsp cornstarch

salt and pepper

3 tbsp all-purpose flour

1½ tbsp butter

1¼ cups milk

¼ cup freshly grated Cheddar cheese

corn oil, for brushing

1 tbsp fresh white bread crumbs

salad leaves, to serve

variation

Use cremini mushrooms instead of the oyster ones and replace the Cheddar cheese with Parmesan cheese, if you prefer.

cook's tip

Oyster mushrooms have a delicate flavor and texture. They are now mostly cultivated so are available from most large supermarkets. Just wipe them with a damp cloth and let dry before using.

1 Place the lasagna sheets in a large, shallow dish. Cover with plenty of boiling water. Cook on HIGH power for 5 minutes. Let stand, covered, for a few minutes before draining. Rinse in cold water and lay the sheets out on a clean counter.

2 Place the onion and butter in a bowl. Cover and cook on HIGH power for 2 minutes. Add the bell pepper, zucchini, and ginger. Cover and cook on HIGH power for 3 minutes. Add the mushrooms and salmon to the bowl. Mix the sherry into the cornstarch, then stir into the bowl. Cover and cook on HIGH power for 4 minutes, or until the fish flakes easily. Add salt and pepper to taste.

3 Whisk the flour, butter, and milk in a bowl. Cook on HIGH power for 3–4 minutes, whisking every minute, to give a sauce of coating consistency. Stir in half the cheese and season to taste with salt and pepper. Spoon the salmon filling in equal quantities along the shorter side of each lasagna sheet. Roll up to enclose the filling.

Oil a large, flameproof rectangular dish. Arrange the rolls in a single layer in the dish, pour over the sauce, and sprinkle over the remaining cheese and bread crumbs.

4 Preheat the broiler. Cook on HIGH power for 3 minutes until heated through. Brown under the broiler before serving with salad.

poached salmon with penne

serves 4 **prep: 10 mins** ☾ **cook: 30 mins** ⏲

Fresh salmon and pasta in a mouthwatering lemon and watercress sauce—a wonderful summer evening treat.

INGREDIENTS

4 fresh salmon steaks (about 9½ oz/ 275 g each)	LEMON & WATERCRESS SAUCE
2 oz/55 g butter	2 tbsp butter
¾ cup dry white wine	3½ tbsp all-purpose flour
pinch of sea salt	⅔ cup warm milk juice, and finely
8 peppercorns	grated rind of 2 lemons
1 fresh dill sprig	2 oz/55 g watercress, chopped
1 fresh tarragon sprig	salt and pepper
1 lemon, sliced	
1 lb/450 g dried penne	TO GARNISH
1 tbsp olive oil	lemon slices
	fresh watercress

NUTRITIONAL INFORMATION

Calories	.968
Protein	.59g
Carbohydrate	.49g
Sugars	.3g
Fat	.58g
Saturates	.19g

variation

You can replace the watercress with the same amount of fresh arugula, if you prefer.

cook's tip

Watercress has a distinctive peppery flavor and should be added toward the end of the cooking time, so the flavor is not lost. It is usually available all year round.

1 Place the salmon in a large, nonstick skillet. Add the butter, wine, sea salt, peppercorns, dill, tarragon, and lemon. Cover, bring to a boil, reduce the heat, and simmer for 10 minutes. Using a spatula, carefully remove the salmon. Strain and reserve the cooking liquid. Remove and discard the salmon skin and center bones. Keep warm.

2 Meanwhile, bring a large, heavy-bottom pan of lightly salted water to a boil. Add the penne, return to a boil, and cook for 8–10 minutes, or until tender but still firm to the bite. Drain thoroughly and sprinkle over the olive oil. Place the penne in a warmed serving dish, top with the salmon steaks and keep warm.

3 To make the sauce, melt the butter and stir in the flour for 2 minutes. Stir in the milk and 7 tablespoons of the reserved cooking liquid. Add the lemon juice and rind, and cook, stirring, for an additional 10 minutes. Add the watercress to the sauce, stir gently, and season to taste with salt and pepper. Pour the sauce over the salmon and penne, garnish with slices of lemon and fresh watercress. Serve immediately.

vegetables & salads

As a combination of pasta and vegetables is both appetizing and attractive, it is a popular choice for everyone, not just vegetarians. Tomatoes, inevitably, take a starring role, and dishes such as Neapolitan Conchiglie (see page 200) and Tagliatelle with Sun-Dried Tomatoes (see page 234) amply demonstrate why. The on-going Italian love affair with mushrooms is also apparent from such mouthwatering classics as Linguine with Exotic Mushrooms (see page 235) and Penne with Creamy Mushrooms (see page 231). Pasta goes superbly with all the typical Mediterranean vegetables—eggplant, zucchini, fennel, pumpkin, olives, beans, bell peppers, and artichokes—and these are featured in sauces and fillings on their own or mixed together in a melt-in-the-mouth medley.

There are dishes for all occasions, whether you are offering guests Saffron Tagliatelle with Asparagus (see page 208) or Casarecci with Artichokes (see page 216); or feeding a hungry family with Vegetable Lasagna (see page 223) or Penne with Mixed Beans (see page 244). Pasta salads are always popular and the perfect choice for entertaining, whether as part of a buffet table or to accompany a barbecue, especially as they can be made in advance. For family meals, they bring a welcome change from lettuce and tomatoes in the summer and a refreshing alternative when salad greens are out of season in the winter. The recipes feature ingredients as diverse as pears, cheese, arugula, nuts, olives, and curry powder, as once again pasta demonstrates its wonderful adaptability.

pasta & vegetable sauce

serves 4   **prep: 15 mins** ⏲   **cook: 20 mins** ⏱

A Mediterranean mixture of red bell peppers, garlic, and zucchini cooked in olive oil, and tossed with pasta.

INGREDIENTS

3 tbsp olive oil

1 onion, sliced

2 garlic cloves, chopped

3 red bell peppers, seeded, and cut into strips

3 zucchini, sliced

14 oz/400 g canned chopped tomatoes

3 tbsp sun-dried tomato paste

2 tbsp chopped fresh basil

salt and pepper

225 g/8 oz fresh fusilli

1 cup freshly grated Gruyère cheese

fresh basil sprigs, to garnish

mixed salad leaves, to serve

variation

Substitute the Gruyère cheese with another hard cheese, such as Emmental. Use ordinary tomato paste if sun-dried is not available.

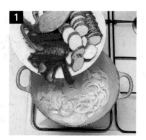

cook's tip

Be careful not to overcook fresh pasta—it should be "al dente" (retaining some "bite"). It takes only a few minutes to cook because it is still full of moisture.

1 Heat the olive oil in a heavy-bottom pan or flameproof casserole. Add the onion and garlic, and cook until softened. Add the peppers and zucchini and cook for 5 minutes, stirring occasionally. Add the tomatoes, sun-dried tomato paste, basil, and salt and pepper to taste. Cover and cook for 5 minutes.

2 Meanwhile, bring a large, heavy-bottom pan of lightly salted water to a boil. Add the pasta, stir, and return to a boil. Reduce the heat slightly and cook, uncovered, for 3 minutes, or until just tender but still firm to the bite. Drain thoroughly and add to the vegetables. Toss gently to mix well.

3 Preheat the broiler to medium. Place the mixture into a shallow ovenproof dish and sprinkle over the cheese. Cook under the broiler for 5 minutes, until the cheese is golden. Garnish with basil sprigs and serve immediately.

pasta & chili tomatoes

prep: 10 mins   cook: 15 mins

The pappardelle and vegetables are tossed in a delicious chili and tomato sauce for a quick and economical meal.

INGREDIENTS

9½ oz/275 g fresh pappardelle

3 tbsp peanut oil

2 garlic cloves, crushed

2 shallots, sliced

8 oz/225 g green beans, sliced

8 cherry tomatoes, halved

1 tsp chili flakes

4 tbsp crunchy peanut butter

⅔ cup coconut milk

1 tbsp tomato paste

sliced scallions,
to garnish

NUTRITIONAL INFORMATION	
Calories 353	
Protein 10g	
Carbohydrate 26g	
Sugars 7g	
Fat 24g	
Saturates 4g	

variation

Add slices of chicken or beef to the recipe and stir-fry with the beans and pasta in Step 3 for a more substantial main meal.

1 Bring a large, heavy-bottom pan of lightly salted water to a boil. Add the pasta, return to a boil, and cook for 5–6 minutes.

2 Heat the peanut oil in a preheated wok or large skillet. Add the garlic and shallots, and stir-fry for 1 minute.

3 Drain the pasta thoroughly. Add the green beans and drained pasta to the wok, and stir-fry for 5 minutes. Add the cherry tomatoes to the wok and mix well.

4 Mix the chili flakes, peanut butter, coconut milk, and tomato paste together in a bowl.

5 Pour the chili mixture over the pasta, toss well to combine, and heat through. Transfer to warmed serving dishes and garnish with sliced scallions. Serve immediately.

chile & pepper pasta

cook: 30 mins

prep: 15 mins, plus 10 mins standing

serves 4

This roasted pepper and chile sauce is sweet and spicy—the perfect combination for any occasion.

NUTRITIONAL INFORMATION

Calories 423

Protein 9g

Carbohydrate 38g

Sugars 5g

Fat 27g

Saturates 4g

INGREDIENTS

2 red bell peppers, halved and seeded

1 small fresh red chile

4 tomatoes, halved

2 garlic cloves

½ cup ground almonds

7 tbsp olive oil

salt

1 lb 8 oz/675 g fresh fusilli or 12 oz/350 g dried fusilli

fresh oregano leaves, to garnish

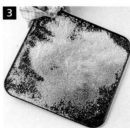

variation

Add 2 tablespoons of red wine vinegar to the sauce and use as a dressing for a cold pasta salad, if you wish.

1 Preheat the broiler. Place the peppers and tomatoes, skin-side up, on a cookie sheet with the chile. Cook under the hot broiler for 10–15 minutes, or until charred. Place the peppers and chile in a plastic bag and let sweat for 10 minutes.

2 Remove the skin from the peppers and chile, and slice the flesh into strips, using a sharp knife. Peel the garlic. Peel and seed the tomatoes.

3 Place the almonds on a cookie sheet and place under the broiler for 2–3 minutes, or until golden.

4 Using a food processor, blend the peppers, chile, garlic, and tomatoes to form a purée. Keep the motor running and slowly add the olive oil to form a thick sauce. Alternatively, mash the mixture with a fork and beat in the olive oil, drop by drop. Stir the toasted ground almonds into the mixture. Warm the sauce in a pan until hot.

5 Bring a large, heavy-bottom pan of lightly salted water to a boil. Add the pasta, return to a boil, and cook for 8–10 minutes if using dried, or 3–5 minutes if using fresh. Drain the pasta thoroughly and transfer to a serving dish. Pour over the sauce and toss to mix. Garnish with the fresh oregano leaves and serve.

pasta with green vegetables

serves 4　　　　　**prep: 10 mins** ⏲　　　　　**cook: 25 mins** ⏲

The different shapes and textures of the vegetables make a mouthwatering presentation in this light and summery dish.

INGREDIENTS

8 oz/225 g dried gemelli or other
pasta shapes
2 tbsp chopped fresh parsley
2 tbsp freshly grated Parmesan cheese

SAUCE
1 head green broccoli, cut into florets
2 zucchini, sliced
8 oz/225 g asparagus spears, trimmed
4½ oz/125 g snow peas
1 cup frozen peas
2 tbsp butter
3 tbsp Vegetable Stock (see page 12)
5 tbsp heavy cream
salt and pepper
large pinch of freshly grated nutmeg

NUTRITIONAL INFORMATION

Calories 517

Protein 17g

Carbohydrate 42g

Sugars 5g

Fat 32g

Saturates 18g

variation

If fresh peas are in season, then they would work well in this recipe. Shell and proceed as in main recipe.

cook's tip

Make sure that the sauce is not boiling when stirring in the cream. If the sauce is too hot it may curdle. Gradually pour in the cream, then heat gently until the sauce is hot.

1 Bring a large, heavy-bottom pan of lightly salted water to a boil. Add the pasta, return to a boil, and cook for 8–10 minutes, or until tender but still firm to the bite. Drain the pasta in a colander, return to the pan, cover, and keep warm.

2 Steam the broccoli, zucchini, asparagus spears, and snow peas over a pan of boiling, salted water until just starting to soften. Remove from the heat and plunge into cold water to prevent further cooking. Drain and reserve. Cook the peas in boiling, salted water for 3 minutes, then drain. Refresh in cold water and drain again.

3 Place the butter and Vegetable Stock in a pan over medium heat. Add all the vegetables, except for the asparagus spears, and toss carefully with a wooden spoon to heat through, taking care not to break them up. Stir in the cream, allow the sauce to heat through, and season to taste with salt, pepper, and nutmeg.

4 Transfer the pasta to a warmed serving dish and stir in the chopped parsley. Spoon the sauce over, and sprinkle on the freshly grated Parmesan. Arrange the asparagus spears in a pattern on top. Serve hot.

tortelloni

serves 4   **prep: 15 mins, plus 5 mins resting**   **cook: 25 mins**

These tasty little squares of pasta stuffed with mushrooms and cheese are surprisingly filling. This recipe makes 36 tortelloni.

INGREDIENTS

10½ oz/300 g Basic Pasta Dough
(see page 13), rolled out
to thin sheets
2¾ oz/75 g butter
½ cup finely chopped shallots
3 garlic cloves, crushed
½ cup wiped and finely
chopped mushrooms

½ celery stalk, finely chopped
½ cup finely grated romano cheese,
plus extra to garnish
salt and pepper

NUTRITIONAL INFORMATION

Calories	.360
Protein	.9g
Carbohydrate	.36g
Sugars	.1g
Fat	.21g
Saturates	.12g

variation

Replace the romano cheese with another hard cheese of your choice, such as Parmesan.

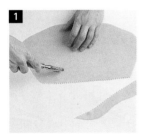

cook's tip

When the tortelloni are cooked they will rise to the surface of the pan. If they are tender but with a slight bite, then they are done.

1 Using a serrated pasta cutter, cut 2-inch/5-cm squares from the sheets of fresh pasta. To make 36 tortelloni you will need 72 squares. Once the pasta is cut, cover the squares with plastic wrap to stop them drying out.

2 Heat 2 tablespoons of the butter in a skillet.

Add the shallots, 1 crushed garlic clove, the mushrooms, and celery, and cook for 4–5 minutes. Remove the skillet from the heat, stir in the cheese and season to taste with salt and pepper.

3 Spoon ½ teaspoon of the mixture onto the center of 36 pasta squares. Brush the edges of the squares

with water and top with the remaining 36 squares. Press the edges together to seal. Let rest for 5 minutes.

4 Bring a large, heavy-bottom pan of water to a boil, add the tortelloni, and cook in batches for 2–3 minutes, or until cooked. Remove with a slotted spoon and drain thoroughly.

5 Meanwhile, melt the remaining butter in a skillet. Add the remaining garlic and plenty of pepper, and cook for 1–2 minutes. Transfer the tortelloni to serving plates and pour over the garlic butter. Garnish with grated romano cheese and serve immediately.

artichoke & olive spaghetti

serves 4   **prep: 20 mins** ⏱   **cook: 35 mins** ⏱

The tasty flavors of artichoke hearts and black olives are definitely a winning combination.

INGREDIENTS

2 tbsp olive oil

1 large red onion, chopped

2 garlic cloves, crushed

1 tbsp lemon juice

4 baby eggplants, quartered

2½ cups strained tomatoes

2 tsp superfine sugar

salt and pepper

2 tbsp tomato paste

14 oz/400 g canned artichoke hearts, drained and halved

⅔ cup pitted black olives

12 oz/350 g whole-wheat dried spaghetti

fresh basil sprigs, to garnish

olive bread, to serve

NUTRITIONAL INFORMATION

Calories 393

Protein 14g

Carbohydrate 63g

Sugars 11g

Fat 11g

Saturates 2g

variation

Replace the 4 baby eggplants with a medium one, cut into chunks. You can use shallots instead of the red onion.

cook's tip

Adding a little sugar with the tomatoes makes the tomatoes sweeter and also brings out their full flavor. If you prefer, omit the sugar and proceed as in main recipe.

1 Heat 1 tablespoon of the oil in a large skillet and gently cook the onion, garlic, lemon juice, and eggplants for 4–5 minutes, or until lightly browned.

2 Pour in the strained tomatoes, season to taste with salt and pepper, and add the sugar and tomato paste. Bring to a boil, reduce the heat, and let simmer for 20 minutes. Gently stir in the artichoke halves and olives, and cook for 5 minutes.

3 Meanwhile, bring a large, heavy-bottom pan of lightly salted water to a boil. Add the spaghetti, return to a boil, and cook for 8–10 minutes, or until just tender, but still firm to the bite.

Drain well, toss in the remaining olive oil, and season to taste with salt and pepper. Transfer the spaghetti to a warmed serving bowl and top with the vegetable sauce. Garnish with basil sprigs and serve with olive bread.

neapolitan conchiglie

serves 4 **prep: 15 mins** ⏱ **cook: 50 mins** ⏱

Naples' most famous daughter, film star Sophia Loren, once remarked that "everything you see I owe to pasta." When you have eaten this classic pasta in tomato sauce, get ready for your screen test!

INGREDIENTS

2 lb/900 g plum tomatoes,
coarsely chopped
⅔ cup dry white wine
1 onion, chopped
1 carrot, chopped
1 celery stalk, chopped
2 fresh flatleaf parsley sprigs
pinch of sugar
salt
12 oz/350 g dried conchiglie
1 tbsp chopped fresh marjoram
freshly grated Parmesan cheese,
to serve

NUTRITIONAL INFORMATION

Calories	385
Protein	13g
Carbohydrate	77g
Sugars	14g
Fat	3g
Saturates	0g

variation

Although fresh plum tomatoes are best for this recipe, you could use 1 lb 12 oz/800 g canned chopped plum tomatoes instead.

1 Place the tomatoes in a large heavy-bottom pan. Add the wine, onion, carrot, celery, parsley, and sugar, and gradually bring to a boil, stirring frequently. Reduce the heat, partially cover, and let simmer, stirring occasionally, for 45 minutes, or until thickened.

2 Meanwhile, bring a large, heavy-bottom pan of lightly salted water to a boil. Add the pasta, return to a boil, and cook for 8–10 minutes, or until tender but still firm to the bite.

3 Rub the tomato sauce through a strainer with the back of a wooden spoon

into a clean pan and stir in the marjoram. Reheat gently, stirring occasionally, for 1–2 minutes. Drain the pasta and transfer to a warmed serving dish. Pour the tomato sauce over the pasta and toss well. Sprinkle with Parmesan cheese and serve immediately with extra grated Parmesan cheese, if you like.

vermicelli with vegetable ribbons

⏱ **cook: 15 mins**　　　⏱ **prep: 15 mins**　　　**serves 4**

*Colorful and tasty, this medley of pasta, vegetables, and fresh herbs
would make a wonderful family lunch on a busy Saturday. Serve
with mixed salad greens and crusty bread, if you like.*

NUTRITIONAL INFORMATION	
Calories	414
Protein	13g
Carbohydrate	73g
Sugars	7g
Fat	10g
Saturates	4g

INGREDIENTS

12 oz/350 g dried vermicelli

3 zucchini

3 carrots

2 tbsp unsalted butter

1 tbsp olive oil

2 garlic cloves, finely chopped

⅜ cup fresh basil, shredded

2 tbsp fresh chives, finely snipped

2 tbsp fresh flatleaf parsley,
finely chopped

salt and pepper

1 small head radicchio, leaves shredded

variation

If you like, you can garnish
the dish with thin shavings
of Parmesan cheese or
crumbled feta cheese.

1 Bring a large heavy-bottom pan of lightly salted water to a boil. Add the pasta, return to a boil, and cook for 8–10 minutes, or until tender but still firm to the bite.

2 Meanwhile, cut the zucchini and carrots into very thin strips with a swivel-blade vegetable peeler or a mandolin. Melt the butter with the olive oil in a heavy-bottom skillet. Add the carrot strips and garlic and cook over low heat, stirring occasionally, for 5 minutes. Add the zucchini strips and all the herbs and season to taste with salt and pepper.

3 Drain the pasta and add it to the skillet. Toss well to mix and cook, stirring occasionally, for 5 minutes. Transfer to a warmed serving dish, add the radicchio, toss well, and serve immediately.

mushroom cannelloni

serves 4　　　　　**prep: 25 mins**　　　　　**cook: 40 mins**

Exotic mushrooms have a rich, earthy flavor that is perfect for this filled pasta dish, but you could use a more economical mixture of exotic and cultivated mushrooms, if you like.

INGREDIENTS

12 dried cannelloni tubes

4 tbsp olive oil, plus extra
for brushing

2 tbsp butter

1 lb/450 g mixed exotic mushrooms,
finely chopped

1 garlic clove, finely chopped

1½ cups fresh bread crumbs

⅔ cup milk

1 cup ricotta cheese

6 tbsp freshly grated Parmesan cheese

salt and pepper

2 tbsp pine nuts

2 tbsp slivered almonds

TOMATO SAUCE

2 tbsp olive oil

1 onion, finely chopped

1 garlic clove, finely chopped

1 lb 12 oz/800 g canned
chopped tomatoes

1 tbsp tomato paste

8 black olives, pitted and chopped

salt and pepper

NUTRITIONAL INFORMATION

Calories	.727
Protein	.26g
Carbohydrate	.59g
Sugars	.14g
Fat	.44g
Saturates	.15g

variation

Substitute half the quantity of exotic mushrooms with exotic cultivated mushrooms, such as shiitake, and ordinary mushrooms like white ones.

cook's tip

Use either a teaspoon or a pastry bag fitted with a large plain tip to fill the canelloni tubes. Do not overfill them.

1 Preheat the oven to 375°F/ 190°C. Bring a large pan of lightly salted water to a boil. Add the cannelloni tubes, return to a boil, and cook for 8–10 minutes, or until tender but still firm to the bite. With a slotted spoon, transfer the cannelloni tubes to a plate and pat dry. Brush a large ovenproof dish with olive oil.

2 Meanwhile, make the tomato sauce. Heat the olive oil in a skillet. Add the onion and garlic and cook over low heat for 5 minutes, or until softened. Add the tomatoes and their can juices, tomato paste, and olives, and season to taste with salt and pepper. Bring to a boil and cook for 3–4 minutes. Pour the sauce into the ovenproof dish.

3 To make the filling, melt the butter in a heavy-bottom skillet. Add the mushrooms and garlic and cook over medium heat, stirring frequently, for 3–5 minutes, or until tender. Remove the skillet from the heat. Mix the bread crumbs, milk, and oil together in a large bowl, then stir in the ricotta, mushroom mixture,

and 4 tablespoons of the Parmesan cheese. Season to taste with salt and pepper.

4 Fill the cannelloni tubes with the mushroom mixture and place them in the dish. Brush with olive oil and sprinkle with the remaining Parmesan cheese, pine nuts, and almonds. Bake in the oven for 25 minutes, or until golden.

pappardelle with pumpkin sauce

⊞ **cook: 1 hr 15 mins**   ↻ **prep: 15 mins**   **serves 4**

NUTRITIONAL INFORMATION

Calories	.580
Protein	.18g
Carbohydrate	.74g
Sugars	.10g
Fat	.26g
Saturates	.16g

variation

If pumpkins are not available, then use other types of squash, such as butternut or acorn squash, instead.

Slow cooking is the key to success with this classic, rich pumpkin sauce which captures the special warmth of the Campania region of southern Italy.

INGREDIENTS

4 tbsp butter

6 shallots, very finely chopped

salt

1 lb 12 oz/800 g pumpkin, peeled, seeded, and cut into pieces

pinch of freshly grated nutmeg

generous ¾ cup light cream

4 tbsp freshly grated Parmesan cheese, plus extra to serve

2 tbsp chopped fresh flatleaf parsley

12 oz/350 g dried pappardelle

cook's tip

To prepare the pumpkin, use a sharp knife to cut it into quarters. Scrape the seeds out with a dessertspoon and discard, then peel and cut the flesh into sticks.

1 Melt the butter in a large heavy-bottom pan. Add the shallots, sprinkle with a little salt, cover, and cook over very low heat, stirring occasionally, for 30 minutes.

2 Add the pumpkin pieces and season to taste with nutmeg. Cover and cook over very low heat,

stirring occasionally, for 40 minutes, or until the pumpkin is pulpy. Stir in the cream, Parmesan cheese, and parsley, and remove the pan from the heat.

3 Meanwhile, bring a large heavy-bottom pan of lightly salted water to a boil. Add the pasta, return to a boil, and cook for 8–10 minutes, or

until tender but still firm to the bite. Drain, reserving 2–3 tablespoons of the cooking water.

4 Add the pasta to the pumpkin mixture and stir in the reserved cooking water if the mixture seems too thick. Cook, stirring constantly, for 1 minute, then transfer to a large, warmed

serving dish and serve immediately with extra grated Parmesan cheese.

fettuccine with bell peppers roman style

serves 4   **prep: 15 mins**   **cook: 40 mins**

Red, yellow, or orange bell peppers are all suitable for this dish, but green bell peppers are a little too sharp in taste and do not provide enough contrast with the saltiness of the olives.

INGREDIENTS

generous ⅓ cup olive oil

1 onion, finely chopped

generous 1 cup black olives, pitted and coarsely chopped

14 oz/400 g canned chopped tomatoes, drained

2 red, yellow, or orange bell peppers, seeded and cut into thin strips

salt and pepper

12 oz/350 g dried fettuccine

freshly grated romano cheese, to serve

NUTRITIONAL INFORMATION

Calories	.555
Protein	.13g
Carbohydrate	.72g
Sugars	.9g
Fat	.26g
Saturates	.4g

cook's tip

Traditionally, tiny black wrinkled olives grown in the Lazio region of Italy are used for this Roman dish, but you could use Spanish or even Greek Kalamata olives, if you like.

1 Heat the olive oil in a large heavy-bottom pan. Add the onion and cook over low heat, stirring occasionally, for 5 minutes, or until softened. Add the olives, tomatoes, and bell peppers, and season to taste with salt and pepper. Cover and let simmer gently over very low heat, stirring occasionally, for 35 minutes.

2 Meanwhile, bring a large heavy-bottom pan of lightly salted water to a boil. Add the pasta, return to a boil, and cook for 8–10 minutes, or until tender but still firm to the bite. Drain the pasta and transfer to a warmed serving dish.

3 Spoon the sauce onto the pasta and toss well. Sprinkle generously with the romano cheese and serve immediately, with extra grated romano cheese.

farfalle with eggplant

cook: 45 mins   **prep: 15 mins**   **serves 4**

This classic combination of eggplants, tomatoes, pasta, and lots of fresh basil is ideal for a quick summer lunch. Any type of short pasta would be suitable for this dish, such as penne or conchiglie.

NUTRITIONAL INFORMATION

Calories	.584
Protein	.12g
Carbohydrate	.72g
Sugars	.9g
Fat	.30g
Saturates	.4g

INGREDIENTS

1 large or 2 medium eggplants, diced

salt and pepper

⅔ cup olive oil

4 shallots, chopped

2 garlic cloves, finely chopped

14 oz/400 g canned chopped tomatoes

1 tsp superfine sugar

12 oz/350 g dried farfalle

fresh basil sprigs, to garnish

cook's tip

While there is no longer the need to salt modern varieties of eggplants to absorb bitter juices, it is still worth doing because it prevents them absorbing a lot of oil during cooking.

1. Place the eggplant in a colander, sprinkling each layer with salt, and let drain for 30 minutes. Meanwhile, heat 1 tablespoon of the olive oil in a heavy-bottom pan. Add the shallots and garlic and cook over low heat, stirring occasionally, for 5 minutes, or until softened. Add the tomatoes and their can juices, stir in the sugar and season to taste with salt and pepper. Cover and let simmer gently, stirring occasionally, for 30 minutes, or until thickened.

2. Rinse the eggplant under cold running water, drain well, and pat dry with paper towels. Heat half the remaining olive oil in a heavy-bottom skillet, then add the eggplant in batches, and cook, stirring frequently, until golden brown all over. Remove from the skillet with a slotted spoon and keep warm while you cook the remaining batches, adding the remaining oil as necessary.

3. Meanwhile, bring a large heavy-bottom pan of lightly salted water to a boil. Add the pasta, return to a boil, and cook for 8–10 minutes, or until tender but still firm to the bite. Drain the pasta and transfer to a warmed serving dish.

4. Pour the tomato sauce over the pasta and toss well to mix. Top with the diced eggplant, garnish with fresh basil sprigs, and serve.

saffron tagliatelle with asparagus

serves 4　　　　　prep: 15 mins 🕒　　　　　cook: 20 mins 🕒

The easy option of serving pasta to vegetarian guests has become something of a cliché, but this is so special that an exception must be made. Cooking the pasta in the same water as the asparagus intensifies the flavor.

INGREDIENTS

pinch of saffron threads	grated rind and juice of ½ lemon
2 tbsp hot water	salt and pepper
1 lb/450 g asparagus spears	scant 1 cup shelled fresh peas
2 tbsp butter	12 oz/350 g dried tagliatelle
1 small onion, finely chopped	2 tbsp chopped fresh chervil
2 tbsp dry white wine	fresh Parmesan cheese shavings
1 cup heavy cream or	
panna da cucina	

NUTRITIONAL INFORMATION

Calories	.656
Protein	17g
Carbohydrate	73g
Sugars	.8g
Fat	.35g
Saturates	.20g

variation

Substitute the chopped fresh chervil with the same amount of shredded fresh basil and use frozen peas if fresh ones are not available.

cook's tip

To make shavings of fresh Parmesan cheese, hold the block of cheese in one hand and use a vegetable peeler to pare off small pieces or shavings into a bowl or over the finished dish.

1 Place the saffron in a small bowl, stir in the hot water, and let soak. Trim off and set aside 2 inches/5 cm of the asparagus tips and slice the remainder.

2 Melt the butter in a heavy-bottom pan. Add the onion and cook over low heat, stirring occasionally, for 5 minutes, or until softened.

Add the wine, cream, and saffron mixture. Bring to a boil, stirring constantly, then reduce the heat and let simmer for 5 minutes, or until slightly thickened. Stir in the lemon rind and juice and season with salt and pepper.

3 Meanwhile, bring a large heavy-bottom pan of lightly salted water to a boil.

Add the reserved asparagus tips and cook for 1 minute. Remove with a slotted spoon and add to the cream sauce. Cook the peas and sliced asparagus in the boiling water for 8 minutes, or until tender. With a slotted spoon, transfer them to the cream sauce. Add the pasta to the water, return to a boil, and cook for 8–10 minutes, or until tender

but still firm to the bite. Drain the pasta and transfer to a warmed serving dish.

4 Add the creamy asparagus sauce, chervil, and Parmesan cheese shavings to the pasta and toss lightly. Serve immediately.

cannelloni in tomato & bell pepper sauce

⏱ **cook: 50 mins**   ⏱ **prep: 25 mins**   **serves 4**

NUTRITIONAL INFORMATION

Calories 822

Protein 23g

Carbohydrate 65g

Sugars 20g

Fat 54g

Saturates 24g

variation

Replace the grated romano cheese with the same amount of freshly grated Parmesan cheese. You can use either white or whole-wheat bread crumbs.

The creamy mascarpone and broccoli filling really does melt in the mouth when you bite into these delicious cannelloni.

INGREDIENTS

12 dried cannelloni tubes

4 tbsp olive oil, plus extra for brushing

1 lb/450 g broccoli, broken into florets

1½ cups fresh bread crumbs

⅔ cup milk

1 cup mascarpone cheese

pinch of grated nutmeg

6 tbsp freshly grated romano cheese

salt and pepper

2 tbsp slivered almonds

TOMATO & BELL PEPPER SAUCE

2 tbsp olive oil

4 shallots, finely chopped

1 garlic clove, finely chopped

1 lb 5 oz/600 g plum tomatoes, peeled, seeded, and chopped

3 red bell peppers, seeded and chopped

1 tbsp sun-dried tomato paste

salt and pepper

1 tbsp shredded basil leaves

cook's tip

To peel tomatoes, use a knife to make a cross in the skin of each tomato. Place in a bowl and pour over enough boiling water to cover and soak for 10 seconds. Drain and rinse, then peel off the skin.

1 Preheat the oven to 375°F/190°C. Bring a large heavy-bottom pan of lightly salted water to a boil. Add the pasta, return to a boil, and cook for 8–10 minutes, or until tender but still firm to the bite. Transfer the pasta to a plate and pat dry with paper towels. Brush a large ovenproof dish with olive oil.

2 Meanwhile, make the sauce. Heat the oil in a skillet. Add the shallots and garlic and cook over low heat for 5 minutes, or until softened. Add the tomatoes, peppers, and sun-dried tomato paste and season with salt and pepper. Bring to a boil, reduce the heat, and let simmer for 20 minutes. Stir in the basil and pour the sauce into the dish.

3 While the sauce is cooking, place the broccoli in a pan of lightly salted boiling water and cook for 10 minutes, or until tender. Drain and let cool slightly, then process to a purée in a food processor. Mix the bread crumbs, milk, and oil together in a large bowl, then stir in the mascarpone cheese, nutmeg, broccoli purée, and

4 tablespoons of the romano cheese. Season to taste with salt and pepper.

4 Fill the cannelloni tubes with the broccoli mixture and place them in the dish. Brush with olive oil and sprinkle with the remaining romano cheese and almonds. Bake in the preheated oven for 25 minutes, or until golden.

tagliatelle with pumpkin

serves 4   **prep: 15 mins**   **cook: 35 mins**

This unusual pasta dish comes from the Emilia Romagna region of Italy. Ideal for a midweek supper dish or dinner party.

INGREDIENTS

1 lb 2 oz/500 g pumpkin

2 tbsp olive oil

1 onion, finely chopped

2 garlic cloves, crushed

4–6 tbsp chopped fresh parsley

salt and pepper

good pinch of freshly grated nutmeg

1 cup Chicken

or Vegetable Stock (see page 12)

4½ oz/125 g prosciutto, cut into

narrow strips

9 oz/275 g tagliatelle, green or white

(fresh or dried)

⅔ cup heavy cream

freshly grated Parmesan cheese,

to serve

NUTRITIONAL INFORMATION

Calories	.454
Protein	.9g
Carbohydrate	.33g
Sugars	.4g
Fat	.33g
Saturates	.12g

variation

If pumpkins are unavailable, then use butternut squash instead. You can also use ground nutmeg instead of grating it yourself.

cook's tip

When buying pumpkins, always choose smaller ones that feel heavy because they will have more flesh than the larger ones.

For a vegetarian option omit the ham.

1 Peel the pumpkin and scoop out the seeds and membrane. Cut the flesh into ½-inch/1-cm dice.

2 Heat the olive oil in a large, heavy-bottom pan and gently cook the onion and garlic until softened. Add half of the parsley and cook for 1–2 minutes. Add the pumpkin and continue to cook for 2–3 minutes. Season well with salt, pepper, and nutmeg.

3 Add half of the stock, bring to a boil, cover, and simmer for 10 minutes, or until the pumpkin is tender, adding more stock as necessary. Add the prosciutto and continue to cook for 2 minutes, stirring frequently.

4 Meanwhile, bring a large, heavy-bottom pan of lightly salted water to a boil. Add the pasta, return to a boil, and cook for 3–4 minutes for fresh pasta, or 8–10 minutes for dried. Drain thoroughly and transfer to a warmed dish. Add the cream to the ham mixture and heat gently. Season to taste with salt and pepper and spoon over the pasta. Sprinkle with the remaining parsley and grated Parmesan cheese separately.

pappardelle with asparagus

serves 4   **prep: 15 mins** ⟳   **cook: 35 mins** ⟳

The first young vegetables of the summer are always a welcome sight. Make the most of them while they are in season.

INGREDIENTS

1 lb 10 oz/750 g asparagus spears

3 oz/85 g butter

1 onion, chopped

2 carrots, chopped

1 celery stalk, chopped

14 oz/400 g canned chopped tomatoes, drained (see Cook's Tip)

salt and pepper

12 oz/350 g dried pappardelle

freshly grated Parmesan cheese, to serve

NUTRITIONAL INFORMATION	
Calories 537
Protein 18g
Carbohydrate 76g
Sugars 13g
Fat 20g
Saturates 12g

cook's tip

Set aside the can juices when you drain the tomatoes. If the mixture seems to be drying out while simmering in Step 2, add a little of the reserved juice.

1 Trim off and set aside about 2 inches/5 cm of the asparagus tips and cut the remainder into 1½-inch/4-cm chunks. Melt the butter in a large heavy-bottom pan. Add the onion, carrots, and celery and cook over low heat, stirring occasionally, for 10 minutes or until the vegetables are softened.

2 Add all the asparagus and cook over low heat for 5 minutes. Add the tomatoes and season to taste with salt and pepper. Cover and let simmer for 20 minutes.

3 Meanwhile, bring a large heavy-bottom pan of lightly salted water to a boil. Add the pasta, return to a boil, and cook for 8–10 minutes, or until tender but still firm to the bite. Drain the pasta and transfer to a warmed serving dish. Spoon the asparagus sauce onto it and toss lightly. Sprinkle with Parmesan cheese and serve immediately.

spaghettini with tomatoes & black olives

cook: 30 mins   **prep: 15 mins**   **serves 4**

This sauce is reminiscent of the classic pizza combination—tomatoes, olives, and capers—with dried chile to add extra interest.

NUTRITIONAL INFORMATION	
Calories	.307
Protein	.11g
Carbohydrate	.51g
Sugars	.11g
Fat	.8g
Saturates	.2g

INGREDIENTS

1 tbsp olive oil

1 garlic clove, finely chopped

2 tsp bottled capers, drained, rinsed and chopped

12 black olives, pitted and chopped

½ dried red chile, crushed

2 lb 12 oz/1.25 kg canned tomatoes

salt

1 tbsp chopped fresh parsley, plus extra to garnish

12 oz/350 g dried spaghettini

2 tbsp freshly grated Parmesan cheese

mixed salad, to serve

cook's tip

Capers are the flower buds of a Mediterranean bush. They are preserved in a mixture of vinegar and salt or in salt alone and should be rinsed before use. Sometimes they are available preserved in olive oil.

1 Heat the olive oil in a large heavy-bottom skillet. Add the garlic and cook over low heat for 30 seconds, then add the capers, olives, dried chile, and tomatoes, and season to taste with salt. Partially cover the pan and let simmer gently for 20 minutes.

2 Stir in the parsley, partially cover the skillet again, and let simmer for an additional 10 minutes.

3 Meanwhile, bring a large heavy-bottom pan of lightly salted water to a boil. Add the pasta, return to a boil, and cook for 8–10 minutes, or until tender but still firm to the bite. Drain and transfer to a warmed serving dish. Add the tomato and olive sauce and toss well. Sprinkle the Parmesan over the pasta and garnish with extra chopped parsley. Serve immediately with a mixed salad.

casarecci with artichokes

serves 4　　　　**prep: 20 mins** ⟲　　　　**cook: 35 mins** ⟳

*Globe artichokes are native to Italy and they still retain a special place
in Italian cuisine. They are associated with many classic Roman dishes.
Here they are combined with that other Italian favorite, fennel.*

INGREDIENTS

2 tbsp lemon juice

2 globe artichokes

2 tbsp olive oil

1 onion, finely chopped

2 garlic cloves, finely chopped

1 fennel bulb, thinly sliced and

feathery fronds set aside

3 tbsp chopped fresh

flatleaf parsley

⅔ cup dry white wine

1 lb 5 oz/600 g plum tomatoes, peeled,

seeded, and chopped

salt and pepper

12 oz/350 g dried casarecci

freshly grated Parmesan cheese,

to serve (optional)

NUTRITIONAL INFORMATION

Calories	.445
Protein	.14g
Carbohydrate	.78g
Sugars	.9g
Fat	.8g
Saturates	.1g

variation

If you cannot find casarecci, then
use dried short-cut macaroni or penne
rigate instead.

cook's tip

Acidulated water prevents the
artichokes from discoloring.
However, they can blacken your
hands when you are preparing
them. To prevent this, rub your
hands with 2 tablespoons
lemon juice before you start.

1 Fill a bowl with cold water and add the lemon juice. Break off the artichoke stalks, then pull off and discard the outer leaves. Cut off the tops of the pale, inner leaves. Cut the bases in half lengthwise and pull out and discard the choke. Thinly slice the artichokes lengthwise, adding the slices to the acidulated water as you go.

2 Heat the olive oil in a large heavy-bottom skillet. Add the chopped onion, garlic, sliced fennel, and parsley, and cook over low heat, stirring frequently, for 8–10 minutes. Pour in the white wine, add the chopped tomatoes, and season to taste with salt and pepper. Cover and let simmer gently for 15 minutes.

3 Meanwhile, bring a large pan of lightly salted water to a boil. Drain the artichokes, then add to the water and cook for 5 minutes. Drain and stir into the skillet. Cover and cook for 10 minutes.

4 Bring a separate large heavy-bottom pan of lightly salted water to a boil.

Add the pasta, return to a boil, and cook for 8–10 minutes, or until tender but still firm to the bite. Drain the pasta and transfer to a warmed serving dish. Add the artichoke sauce and toss. Garnish with the reserved fennel fronds and serve immediately with Parmesan cheese, if you like.

ziti with arugula

serves 4   **prep: 10 mins**   **cook: 12 mins**

Now a city restaurant favorite, this was once a peasant dish from Calabria, where arugula grows wild. It is traditionally made with ziti, wide pasta tubes, which may be smooth or ridged, but you could use elbow macaroni instead, if you like.

INGREDIENTS

12 oz/350 g dried ziti, broken into
1½-inch/4-cm lengths

5 tbsp extra virgin olive oil

2 garlic cloves, lightly crushed

4¼ cups arugula

2 fresh red chiles, thickly sliced

freshly grated romano cheese,
to serve

NUTRITIONAL INFORMATION

Calories 439

Protein 12g

Carbohydrate 66g

Sugars 4g

Fat 16g

Saturates 2g

variation

Substitute the arugula with the same amount of baby spinach leaves and replace the romano with Parmesan.

1 Bring a large heavy-bottom pan of lightly salted water to a boil. Add the pasta, return to a boil, and cook for 8–10 minutes, or until tender but still firm to the bite.

2 Meanwhile, heat the olive oil in a large heavy-bottom skillet. Add the garlic, arugula, and chiles, and stir-fry for 5 minutes, or until the arugula has wilted.

3 Stir 2 tablespoons of the pasta cooking water into the arugula, then drain the pasta and add to the skillet. Cook, stirring frequently, for 2 minutes, then transfer to a warmed serving dish. Remove and discard the garlic cloves and chiles and serve immediately with the romano cheese.

cook's tip

Wild arugula has a more pungent, peppery flavor than the cultivated variety. However, if you find it is too strong, blanch the leaves for 1 minute in boiling water and pat dry before stir-frying.

macaroni with roasted vegetables

🕒 **cook: 40 mins**   🕒 **prep: 20 mins**   **serves 4**

NUTRITIONAL INFORMATION	
Calories	530
Protein	16g
Carbohydrate	88g
Sugars	18g
Fat	16g
Saturates	2g

Roasting Mediterranean vegetables brings out their sweetness and full flavor to make a naturally rich sauce for pasta.

INGREDIENTS

2 onions, cut into wedges

2 zucchini, cut into chunks

1 red bell pepper, seeded and cut into chunks

1 yellow bell pepper, seeded and cut into chunks

1 eggplant, cut into chunks

1 lb/450 g plum tomatoes, quartered and seeded

3 garlic cloves, chopped

4 tbsp olive oil

salt and pepper

12 oz/350 g dried short-cut macaroni

1¼ cups strained tomatoes

½ cup black olives, pitted and halved

GARNISH

fresh basil sprigs

fresh flatleaf parsley sprigs

variation

Other vegetables would work well in this dish, such as red onions, bite-size pieces of butternut squash and cherry tomato halves.

cook's tip

When buying fresh tomatoes, always choose ones that are firm and bright red. Ripe tomatoes can be stored in the refrigerator for up to 2 days, and underripe ones should be kept at room temperature.

1 Preheat the oven to 475°F/240°C. Spread out the onions, zucchini, red and yellow bell peppers, eggplant, and tomatoes in a single layer in a large roasting pan. Sprinkle with the garlic, drizzle with the olive oil, and season to taste with salt and pepper. Stir well until all the vegetables are coated. Roast in the preheated oven for

15 minutes, then remove from the oven and stir well. Return to the oven for an additional 15 minutes.

2 Bring a large heavy-bottom pan of lightly salted water to a boil. Add the pasta, return to a boil, and cook for 8–10 minutes, or until tender but still firm to the bite.

3 Meanwhile, transfer the roasted vegetables to a large heavy-bottom pan and add the strained tomatoes and olives. Heat through gently, stirring occasionally. Drain the pasta and transfer to a warmed serving dish. Add the roasted vegetable sauce and toss well. Garnish with the fresh basil and parsley and serve immediately.

vegetable lasagna

⏱ **cook: 45–55 mins**   ⏱ **prep: 25 mins**   **serves 4**

NUTRITIONAL INFORMATION

Calories	.930
Protein	.35g
Carbohydrate	.60g
Sugars	.18g
Fat	.62g
Saturates	.28g

variation

Replace the zucchini with 4 red bell peppers, cut into strips and cooked in the grill pan. Substitute the plain lasagna with spinach-flavored lasagna.

Layers of pasta, Mediterranean vegetables, mozzarella cheese, and a creamy sauce would make a substantial and delicious vegetarian main dish at any time of year.

INGREDIENTS

olive oil, for brushing

2 eggplants, sliced

2 tbsp butter

1 garlic clove, finely chopped

4 zucchini, sliced

1 tbsp finely chopped fresh flatleaf parsley

1 tbsp finely chopped fresh marjoram

8 oz/225 g mozzarella cheese, grated

2½ cups strained tomatoes

6 oz/175 g dried no-precook lasagna

salt and pepper

2½ cups Béchamel Sauce (see page 12)

½ cup freshly grated Parmesan cheese

cook's tip

Make sure that the oiled grill pan is very hot before adding the eggplant slices. Add extra oil if the eggplants are sticking to the pan.

1 Preheat the oven to 400°F/200°C. Brush a large ovenproof dish with olive oil. Brush a large grill pan with olive oil and heat until smoking. Add half the eggplants and cook over medium heat for 8 minutes, or until golden brown all over. Remove from the grill pan and drain on paper towels. Add the remaining eggplant slices and extra oil, if necessary, and cook for 8 minutes, or until golden brown all over.

2 Melt the butter in a skillet and add the garlic, zucchinis, parsley, and marjoram. Cook over medium heat for 5 minutes, or until the zucchini are golden brown. Remove from the skillet and let drain on paper towels.

3 Layer the eggplants, zucchini, grated mozzarella, strained tomatoes, and lasagna in the dish, seasoning with salt and pepper as you go and finishing with a layer of lasagna. Pour over the Béchamel Sauce, making sure that all the pasta is covered. Sprinkle with the grated Parmesan cheese and bake in the preheated oven for 30–40 minutes, or until golden brown. Serve immediately.

basil & pine nut pesto

serves 4   **prep: 15 mins**   **cook: 10 mins**

Delicious stirred into pasta, soups, and salad dressings, pesto is available in most supermarkets, but making your own gives a concentrated flavor.

INGREDIENTS

about 40 fresh basil leaves

3 garlic cloves, crushed

¼ cup pine nuts

½ cup finely grated
Parmesan cheese

2–3 tbsp extra virgin olive oil

salt and pepper

1 lb 8 oz/675 g fresh pasta or
12 oz/350 g dried pasta

NUTRITIONAL INFORMATION

Calories 321

Protein 11g

Carbohydrate 32g

Sugars 1g

Fat 17g

Saturates 4g

cook's tip

Only buy pine nuts in small quantities—they quickly turn rancid because they have a high oil content. Pine nuts are available in most large supermarkets or health food stores.

1 Rinse the basil leaves and pat them dry with paper towels.

2 Place the basil leaves, garlic, pine nuts, and grated Parmesan cheese into a food processor and blend for 30 seconds, or until smooth. Alternatively, pound all of the ingredients by hand, using a mortar and pestle.

3 If you are using a food processor, keep the motor running and slowly add the olive oil. Alternatively, add the oil drop by drop while stirring briskly. Season to taste with salt and pepper.

4 Bring a large, heavy-bottom pan of water to a boil. Add the pasta, return to a boil, and cook for

3–4 minutes for fresh pasta, or 8–10 minutes for dried, until tender but still firm to the bite. Drain the pasta thoroughly, then transfer the pasta to a serving plate and serve with the pesto. Toss to mix well and serve hot.

pasta with cheese & broccoli

⏲ **cook: 15 mins**   ⏱ **prep: 5 mins**   **serves 4**

Some of the simplest and most satisfying dishes are made with pasta, such as this delicious combination of tagliatelle with two-cheese sauce.

NUTRITIONAL INFORMATION	
Calories	.624
Protein	.22g
Carbohydrate	.34g
Sugars	.2g
Fat	.45g
Saturates	.28g

INGREDIENTS

10½ oz/300 g dried tagliatelle tricolore

8 oz/225 g broccoli, broken into
small florets

12 oz/350g mascarpone cheese

4½ oz/125 g blue cheese, chopped

1 tbsp chopped fresh oregano

2 tbsp butter

salt and pepper

fresh oregano sprigs, to garnish

freshly grated Parmesan cheese,
to serve

cook's tip

When buying blue cheese, always choose cheese with a firm rind and avoid all cheese that has a smell of ammonia. If possible, taste before you buy.

1 Bring a large, heavy-bottom pan of lightly salted water to a boil. Add the pasta, return to a boil, and cook for 8–10 minutes, or until just tender but still firm to the bite.

2 Meanwhile, cook the broccoli florets in a small amount of lightly salted, boiling water. Avoid overcooking the broccoli, so that it retains much of its color and texture.

3 Heat the mascarpone and blue cheeses together gently in a large pan until melted. Stir in the oregano and season to taste with salt and pepper.

4 Drain the pasta thoroughly. Return it to the pan and add the butter, tossing the pasta to coat it. Drain the broccoli well and add to the pasta with the sauce, tossing gently to mix. Divide the pasta between 4 warmed plates. Garnish with oregano sprigs and serve with grated Parmesan cheese.

mixed vegetable agnolotti

serves 4   **prep: 25 mins** ⟳   **cook: 45–50 mins** ⟳

These little pasta circles are filled with such a succulent combination of vegetables that no extra sauce is required. Serve with mixed salad greens or a tomato and onion salad.

INGREDIENTS

butter, for greasing
1 quantity Basic Pasta Dough
(see page 13)
all-purpose flour, for dusting
¾ cup freshly grated
Parmesan cheese

FILLING
½ cup olive oil
1 red onion, chopped
3 garlic cloves, chopped

2 large eggplants, cut into chunks
3 large zucchini, cut into chunks
6 beefsteak tomatoes, peeled, seeded, and coarsely chopped
1 large green bell pepper, seeded and diced
1 large red bell pepper, seeded and diced
1 tbsp sun-dried tomato paste
1 tbsp shredded fresh basil
salt and pepper

NUTRITIONAL INFORMATION	
Calories	.684
Protein	.23g
Carbohydrate	.59g
Sugars	.15g
Fat	.42g
Saturates	.10g

variation

You can use this filling for most pasta shapes, such as ravioli (see page 101) or tortellini (see page 118).

cook's tip

If the filling seems too sloppy after cooking, boil uncovered for 1–2 minutes to reduce slightly. Make sure that any unused dough is covered with a dish towel to prevent it drying out.

1 Preheat the oven to 400°F/200°C. To make the filling, heat the olive oil in a large heavy-bottom pan. Add the onion and garlic and cook over low heat, stirring occasionally, for 5 minutes, or until softened. Add the eggplants, zucchini, tomatoes, green and red bell peppers, sun-dried tomato paste, and basil. Season to taste with salt and pepper, cover and let simmer gently, stirring occasionally, for 20 minutes.

2 Lightly grease an ovenproof dish with butter. Roll out the Pasta Dough on a lightly floured counter and stamp out 3-inch/7.5-cm circles with a plain pastry cutter. Place a spoonful of the vegetable filling on each circle. Dampen the edges slightly and fold the pasta circles over, pressing together to seal.

3 Bring a large pan of lightly salted water to a boil. Add the agnolotti, in batches if necessary, return to a boil and cook for 3–4 minutes. Remove with a slotted spoon, drain, and transfer to the dish. Sprinkle with the Parmesan cheese and bake in the preheated oven for 20 minutes. Serve immediately.

spinach & ricotta ravioli

serves 4 **prep: 25 mins, plus ↻ 1 hr resting** **cook: 15 mins ⊞**

A favorite Italian combination, spinach and ricotta appears in many guises from roulades to crêpes, but it is never more delicious than as a filling for homemade pasta.

INGREDIENTS

12 oz/350 g fresh spinach leaves, coarse stalks removed

generous 1 cup ricotta cheese

½ cup freshly grated Parmesan cheese

1 egg, lightly beaten

pinch of freshly grated nutmeg

pepper

1 quantity Spinach Pasta Dough (see page 13)

all-purpose flour, for dusting

TO SERVE

freshly grated Parmesan cheese

Cheese Sauce (see page 42) or Tomato & Red Bell Pepper Sauce (see page 211)

NUTRITIONAL INFORMATION

Calories	.434
Protein	.25g
Carbohydrate	.42g
Sugars	.4g
Fat	.19g
Saturates	.8g

variation

Replace the Spinach Pasta Dough with either plain or tomato-flavored dough and add 1 tablespoon of chopped fresh parsley to the filling in Step 2.

cook's tip

When cutting the ravioli into squares, use a special pasta cutter available from specialist kitchenware stores. Alternatively, you can use a sharp knife.

1 To make the filling, place the spinach in a heavy-bottom pan with just the water clinging to the leaves after washing, then cover and cook over low heat for 5 minutes, or until wilted. Drain well and squeeze out as much moisture as possible. Let cool, then chop finely.

2 Beat the ricotta cheese until smooth, then stir in the spinach, Parmesan cheese, and egg, and season to taste with nutmeg and pepper.

3 Divide the Pasta Dough in half and roll out on a lightly floured counter. Make the ravioli (see page 101, Step 2), filling them with the

spinach and ricotta mixture. Cut the ravioli into squares and place on a floured dish towel. Let rest for 1 hour.

4 Bring a large heavy-bottom pan of lightly salted water to a boil, add the ravioli, in batches, return to a boil, and cook for 5 minutes. Remove with a slotted spoon

and drain on paper towels. Transfer to a warmed serving dish and serve immediately, sprinkled with Parmesan cheese and/or a sauce, if you like.

penne with creamy mushrooms

cook: 20 mins   **prep: 10 mins**   **serves 4**

NUTRITIONAL INFORMATION

Calories 780

Protein 15g

Carbohydrate 71g

Sugars 7g

Fat 50g

Saturates 21g

variation

Replace the shallots with a small onion, sliced, and substitute the pasta with other short pasta, such as farfalle, fusilli, or rigatoni.

This quick and easy dish would make a wonderful midweek supper, whether or not you are a vegetarian family. Serve with fresh ciabatta, if you like.

INGREDIENTS

4 tbsp butter

1 tbsp olive oil

6 shallots, sliced

1 lb/450 g cremini mushrooms, sliced

salt and pepper

1 tsp all-purpose flour

⅔ cup heavy cream or panna da cucina

2 tbsp port

4 oz/115 g sun-dried tomatoes in oil, drained and chopped

pinch of freshly grated nutmeg

12 oz/350 g dried penne

2 tbsp chopped fresh flatleaf parsley

cook's tip

Nutmeg is used widely in Italian cooking as it has a fragrant, sweet aroma. Use freshly grated nutmeg rather than ground, which rapidly deteriorates. Store nutmeg in an airtight container.

1 Melt the butter with the olive oil in a large heavy-bottom skillet. Add the shallots and cook over low heat, stirring occasionally, for 4–5 minutes, or until softened. Add the mushrooms and cook over low heat for an additional 2 minutes. Season to taste with salt and pepper, sprinkle in the flour and cook, stirring, for 1 minute.

2 Remove the skillet from the heat and gradually stir in the cream and port. Return to the heat, add the sun-dried tomatoes, and grated nutmeg, and cook over low heat, stirring occasionally, for 8 minutes.

3 Meanwhile, bring a large heavy-bottom pan of lightly salted water to a boil.

Add the pasta, return to a boil, and cook for 8–10 minutes, or until tender but still firm to the bite. Drain the pasta well and add to the mushroom sauce. Cook for 3 minutes, then transfer to a warmed serving dish. Sprinkle with the chopped parsley and serve immediately.

vegetable pasta nests

serves 4   prep: 25 mins ⟲   cook: 40 mins ⟳

These large pasta nests look impressive when presented filled with grilled mixed vegetables, and taste delicious.

INGREDIENTS

6 oz/175 g dried spaghetti

1 eggplant, halved and sliced

1 zucchini, diced

1 red bell pepper, seeded and chopped diagonally

6 tbsp olive oil

2 garlic cloves, crushed

4 tbsp butter or margarine, melted plus extra for greasing

1 tbsp dry white bread crumbs

salt and pepper

fresh flatleaf parsley sprigs, to garnish

variation

Replace the red bell pepper with a yellow or orange one and use whole-wheat bread crumbs instead of white.

cook's tip

Serve these nests at a dinner party as an impressive appetizer or as a colorful side-dish to accompany a broiled fish, meat or poultry dish.

1 Preheat the oven to 400°F/200°C. Bring a large heavy-bottom pan of water to a boil. Add the spaghetti, return to a boil, and cook for 8–10 minutes, or until tender but still firm to the bite. Drain the spaghetti and set aside.

2 Preheat the broiler. Place the eggplant,

zucchini, and bell pepper on a cookie sheet. Mix the oil and garlic together and pour over the vegetables, tossing to coat all over. Cook under the hot broiler for 10 minutes, turning, until tender and lightly charred. Keep warm.

3 Divide the spaghetti into 4 on a lightly greased cookie sheet. Using

2 forks, curl the spaghetti to form nests. Brush the pasta nests with melted butter and sprinkle with the bread crumbs. Bake in the preheated oven for 15 minutes, or until lightly golden. Remove the pasta nests from the cookie sheet and transfer to serving plates. Divide the broiled vegetables between the pasta nests, season to taste with salt

and pepper, and garnish with parsley sprigs.

tagliatelle with sun-dried tomatoes

serves 4   **prep: 10 mins**   **cook: 10 mins**

Quick, easy, utterly delicious, and full of sunshine colors and flavors, this is the perfect dish for any occasion, whether it is a family supper or an informal dinner party.

INGREDIENTS

12 oz/350 g dried tagliatelle

1 tbsp olive oil

2 pieces of sun-dried tomatoes in oil, drained and thinly sliced

2 tbsp sun-dried tomato paste

1 cup dry white wine

2 oz/55 g radicchio leaves, shredded

salt and pepper

3 scallions, thinly sliced

3 tbsp lightly toasted pine nuts

NUTRITIONAL INFORMATION

Calories 494

Protein 13g

Carbohydrate 68g

Sugars 5g

Fat 17g

Saturates 2g

cook's tip

To toast pine nuts, place them in a heavy-bottom or nonstick dry skillet and cook over medium heat, stirring and tossing constantly, for 1–2 minutes, until golden.

1 Bring a large heavy-bottom pan of lightly salted water to a boil. Add the pasta, return to a boil, and cook for 8–10 minutes, or until tender but still firm to the bite.

2 Meanwhile, heat half the olive oil in a large heavy-bottom skillet. Add the tomatoes and sun-dried tomato paste and stir in the wine. Let simmer over low heat, stirring constantly, or until slightly reduced. Stir in the radicchio and season to taste with salt and pepper.

3 Drain the pasta and transfer to a warmed serving dish. Add the remaining olive oil and toss well with 2 forks. Top with the sun-dried tomato sauce and toss lightly again, then sprinkle with the scallions and toasted pine nuts and serve immediately.

linguine with exotic mushrooms

⏱ **cook: 20 mins**   ⏲ **prep: 15 mins**   **serves 4**

Use any combination of your favorite mushrooms, such as chanterelles, portobello, oyster, and cremini, or use just one well-flavored variety, such as cèpes, horn of plenty, or hedgehog fungus.

NUTRITIONAL INFORMATION

Calories 600

Protein 19g

Carbohydrate 72g

Sugars 5g

Fat 28g

Saturates 17g

INGREDIENTS

4 tbsp butter

1 onion, chopped

1 garlic clove, finely chopped

12 oz/350 g exotic mushrooms, sliced

12 oz/350 g dried linguine

1¼ cups sour cream

2 tbsp shredded fresh basil leaves, plus extra to garnish

4 tbsp freshly grated Parmesan cheese, plus extra to serve

salt and pepper

cook's tip

If you pick exotic mushrooms yourself, make sure that you can identify them correctly, as many inedible or even toxic mushrooms closely resemble a number of edible varieties.

1 Melt the butter in a large heavy-bottom skillet. Add the onion and garlic and cook over low heat for 5 minutes, or until softened. Add the mushrooms and cook, stirring occasionally, for an additional 10 minutes.

2 Meanwhile, bring a large heavy-bottom pan of lightly salted water to a boil. Add the pasta, return to a boil, and cook for 8–10 minutes, or until tender but still firm to the bite.

3 Stir the sour cream, basil, and Parmesan cheese into the mushroom mixture and season to taste with salt and pepper. Cover and heat through gently for 1–2 minutes. Drain the pasta and transfer to a warmed serving dish. Add the mushroom mixture and toss lightly. Garnish with extra basil and serve immediately with extra Parmesan cheese.

tagliatelle with garlic butter

serves 4 **prep: 25 mins, plus 15 mins resting** **cook: 5 mins**

Pasta is not difficult to make yourself, just a little time-consuming. The resulting pasta only takes a couple of minutes to cook and tastes wonderful.

INGREDIENTS

3½ cups white bread flour, plus extra for dusting

2 tsp salt

4 eggs, beaten

2 tbsp olive oil

2¾ oz/75 g butter, melted

3 garlic cloves, finely chopped

2 tbsp chopped fresh parsley

pepper

NUTRITIONAL INFORMATION

Calories 642

Protein 16g

Carbohydrate 84g

Sugars 2g

Fat 29g

Saturates 13g

variation

You don't have to make tagliatelle for this recipe. You can make any type of pasta you wish.

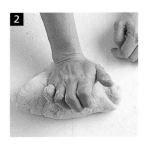

cook's tip

If you prefer, use a pasta machine to make the pasta, but be aware that while the results are usually neater and thinner than hand-made they are not necessarily better.

1 Sift the flour into a large bowl and stir in the salt. Make a well in the center of the dry ingredients and add the eggs and the olive oil. Using a wooden spoon, stir in the eggs, gradually drawing in the flour. After a few minutes the dough will be too stiff to use a spoon and you will need to use your fingers.

2 Once all of the flour has been incorporated, turn the dough out on a floured counter and knead for 5 minutes, or until smooth and elastic. If the dough is too wet, add a little more flour and continue kneading. Cover with plastic wrap and let rest for at least 15 minutes.

3 Roll out the pasta thinly and cut the pasta shapes required. This can be done by hand or using a pasta machine. To make the tagliatelle by hand, fold the thinly rolled pasta sheets into 3 and cut out long, thin strips, ½-inch/1-cm wide.

4 To cook, bring a large, heavy-bottom pan of water to a boil. Add the pasta, return to a boil, and cook for 2–3 minutes, or until tender but still firm to the bite. Drain.

5 Mix the butter, garlic, and parsley together. Stir into the pasta, season with a little pepper to taste and serve immediately.

spicy tomato tagliatelle

serves 4   **prep: 15 mins** ↳   **cook: 35 mins** ⏲

A deliciously fresh and slightly spicy tomato sauce, which is excellent for lunch or a light supper dish.

INGREDIENTS

4 tbsp butter

1 onion, finely chopped

1 garlic clove, crushed

2 small fresh red chiles, seeded and diced

1 lb/450 g fresh tomatoes, peeled, seeded and diced

¾ cup Vegetable Stock (see page 12)

2 tbsp tomato paste

1 tsp sugar

salt and pepper

1 lb 8 oz/675 g fresh green and white tagliatelle, or 12 oz/350 g dried

NUTRITIONAL INFORMATION

Calories 306

Protein 8g

Carbohydrate 45g

Sugars 7g

Fat 12g

Saturates 7g

variation

Try topping your pasta dish with 1¾ oz/50 g pancetta or unsmoked bacon, diced and dry-fried for 5 minutes, or until crispy.

cook's tip

After handling fresh chiles, always wash your hands, knife, and cutting board thoroughly and never let any part of the chile go near your eyes, mouth, or nose. If you prefer, wear rubber gloves.

1 Melt the butter in a large pan. Add the onion and garlic, and cook for 3–4 minutes, or until softened. Add the chiles to the pan and continue cooking for 2 minutes.

2 Add the tomatoes and stock, reduce the heat, and let simmer for 10 minutes, stirring.

3 Pour the sauce into a food processor and blend for 1 minute until smooth. Alternatively, push the sauce through a strainer.

4 Return the sauce to the pan and add the tomato paste, sugar, and salt and pepper to taste. Gently reheat over low heat, until piping hot.

5 Bring a large, heavy-bottom pan of lightly salted water to a boil. Add the pasta, return to a boil, and cook for 8–10 minutes, or until tender, but still firm to the bite. Drain the tagliatelle, transfer to serving plates, and serve with the tomato sauce.

olive, pepper & cherry tomato pasta

serves 4   **prep: 10 mins**   **cook: 25 mins**

The sweet cherry tomatoes in this recipe add color and flavor and are complemented by the black olives and bell peppers.

INGREDIENTS

8 oz/225 g dried penne

2 tbsp olive oil

2 tbsp butter

2 garlic cloves, crushed

1 green bell pepper, seeded and
thinly sliced

1 yellow bell pepper, seeded and
thinly sliced

16 cherry tomatoes, halved

1 tbsp chopped fresh oregano

½ cup dry white wine

2 tbsp quartered, pitted black olives

salt and pepper

2¾ oz/75 g arugula

fresh oregano sprigs, to garnish

NUTRITIONAL INFORMATION

Calories 380

Protein 8g

Carbohydrate 48g

Sugars 6g

Fat 16g

Saturates 7g

---

variation

If arugula is unavailable, spinach makes a good substitute. Follow the same cooking instructions as for arugula.

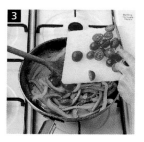

cook's tip

Cherry tomatoes have a sweet delicate flavor and there are numerous different varieties available, including miniature plum tomatoes. Store cherry tomatoes for up to 2 weeks in the refrigerator.

1 Bring a large, heavy-bottom pan of lightly salted water to a boil. Add the pasta, return to a boil, and cook for 8–10 minutes, or until tender but still firm to the bite. Drain the pasta thoroughly.

2 Heat the oil and butter in a skillet until the butter melts. Cook the garlic for 30 seconds. Add the peppers and cook, stirring constantly, for 3–4 minutes.

3 Stir in the cherry tomatoes, oregano, wine, and olives, and cook for 3–4 minutes. Season well with salt and pepper and stir in the arugula until just wilted. Transfer the pasta to a serving dish, spoon over the sauce, and garnish with oregano sprigs. Serve.

pasta & bean casserole

serves 4   **prep: 25 mins** ⌛   **cook: 3 hrs 30 mins** ⏲

*A satisfying winter dish, this is a slow-cooked, one-pot pasta meal.
The beans need to be soaked overnight, so prepare well in advance.*

INGREDIENTS

1⅓ cups dried Great Northern beans,
soaked overnight and drained

8 oz/225 g dried penne

6 tbsp olive oil

3½ cups Vegetable Stock (see page 12)

2 large onions, sliced

2 garlic cloves, chopped

2 bay leaves

1 tsp dried oregano

1 tsp dried thyme

5 tbsp red wine

2 tbsp tomato paste

2 celery stalks, sliced

1 fennel bulb, sliced

4 oz/115 g mushrooms, sliced

8 oz/225 g tomatoes, sliced

1 tsp dark muscovado sugar

2 oz/55 g dry white bread crumbs

salt and pepper

TO SERVE

salad leaves

crusty bread

variation

If penne is unavailable you can substitute almost any variety of short pasta for this dish, such as rigatoni, fusilli, or shell-shaped conchiglie.

cook's tip

Do not be tempted to cook the pasta for more than 2–3 minutes before adding to the casserole so that it keeps its shape and texture during the rest of the cooking time.

1 Preheat the oven to 350°F/180°C. Put the beans in a large pan, add water to cover and bring to a boil. Boil the beans rapidly for 20 minutes, then drain them and set aside.

2 Cook the pasta for 3 minutes in a large pan of boiling salted water, adding 1 tablespoon of the

olive oil. Drain in a colander and set aside.

3 Put the beans in a large flameproof casserole, pour in the vegetable stock and stir in the remaining olive oil, the onions, garlic, bay leaves, herbs, red wine, and tomato paste.

4 Bring to a boil, cover the casserole, and cook in the preheated oven for 2 hours.

5 Remove the casserole from the oven and add the reserved pasta, the celery, fennel, mushrooms, and tomatoes and season to taste with salt and pepper. Stir in the sugar and sprinkle the

bread crumbs on top. Cover the casserole again, return to the oven, and continue cooking for 1 hour. Serve with salad leaves and crusty bread.

penne with mixed beans

This is a useful—and versatile—pantry dish that makes a filling and delicious meal for both vegetarians and vegans, which can be whipped up in only a matter of minutes.

INGREDIENTS

1 tbsp olive oil

1 onion, chopped

1 garlic clove, finely chopped

1 carrot, finely chopped

1 celery stalk, finely chopped

15 oz/425 g canned mixed beans, drained and rinsed

1 cup strained tomatoes

1 tbsp chopped fresh chervil, plus extra leaves to garnish

salt and pepper

12 oz/350 g dried penne

NUTRITIONAL INFORMATION

Calories	.366
Protein	.14g
Carbohydrate	.72g
Sugars	.7g
Fat	.5g
Saturates	.0g

variation

Most canned beans, with the exception of lentils, could be used separately or in combination. Try cranberry, red kidney beans, or chickpeas.

1 Heat the olive oil in a large heavy-bottom skillet. Add the onion, garlic, carrot, and celery, and cook over low heat, stirring occasionally, for 5 minutes, or until the onion has softened.

2 Add the mixed beans, strained tomatoes, and chopped chervil to the skillet and season the mixture to taste with salt and pepper. Cover and let simmer gently for 15 minutes.

3 Meanwhile, bring a large heavy-bottom pan of lightly salted water to a boil. Add the pasta, return to a boil, and cook for 8–10 minutes, or until tender but still firm to the bite. Drain the pasta and transfer to a warmed serving dish. Add the mixed bean sauce, toss well, and serve immediately, garnished with extra chervil.

tagliarini with zucchini

⏱ **cook: 25 mins**   ⏲ **prep: 15 mins**   **serves 4**

This dish is ideal to serve on a hot summer's day as it is full of the sunshine flavors of the Mediterranean. You can serve the Parmesan cheese separately so everyone can help themselves.

NUTRITIONAL INFORMATION	
Calories	555
Protein	. . . . .22g
Carbohydrate	. . . . .77g
Sugars	. . . . .7g
Fat	. . . . .20g
Saturates	. . . . .6g

INGREDIENTS

4 tbsp olive oil

1 red onion, chopped

1 garlic clove, finely chopped

1 lb 2 oz/500 g zucchini, diced

2 beefsteak tomatoes, peeled, seeded, and finely chopped

salt

pinch of cayenne pepper

1 tbsp shredded fresh basil leaves

12 oz/350 g dried tagliarini

¾ cup freshly grated

Parmesan cheese, to serve

variation

Use spaghetti instead of the tagliarini and replace the basil with the same amount of chopped fresh flatleaf parsley.

1 Heat the oil in a large heavy-bottom skillet. Add the onion and garlic and cook over low heat, stirring occasionally, for 5 minutes, or until softened. Add the zucchinis and cook, stirring, for an additional 3 minutes.

2 Add the tomatoes and season to taste with salt and cayenne pepper. Stir in the basil, cover, and cook for 10–15 minutes, or until all the vegetables are tender.

3 Meanwhile, bring a large heavy-bottom pan of lightly salted water to a boil. Add the pasta, return to a boil, and cook for 8–10 minutes, or until tender but still firm to the bite. Drain the pasta and transfer to a warmed serving dish. Add the zucchini and tomato sauce and toss well. Sprinkle with the Parmesan cheese and serve immediately.

orecchiette salad with pears & stilton

serves 4   **prep: 15 mins** ⏲   **cook: 10 mins** ⏱

*A classic combination in British cooking, pears and blue cheese,
form the basis of this unusual salad, which could serve as a main
course for four people or as an appetizer for six.*

INGREDIENTS

9 oz/250 g dried orecchiette	1 red onion, sliced
1 head of radicchio, torn into pieces	1 carrot, grated
1 oak leaf lettuce, torn into pieces	8 fresh basil leaves
2 pears	2 oz/55 g corn salad
3 tbsp lemon juice	4 tbsp olive oil
9 oz/250 g Stilton cheese, diced	3 tbsp white wine vinegar
scant ½ cup chopped walnuts	salt and pepper
4 tomatoes, quartered	

NUTRITIONAL INFORMATION

Calories 766

Protein 27g

Carbohydrate 66g

Sugars 19g

Fat 46g

Saturates 17g

variation

Substitute the oak leaf lettuce with
escarole and replace the corn salad with
arugula or watercress, if you prefer.

cook's tip

The easiest way to emulsify an
oil and vinegar dressing is to
put the ingredients in a screw-
top jar, secure the lid, and
shake vigorously. Otherwise,
whisk well in a bowl or pitcher.

1 Bring a large heavy-
bottom pan of lightly
salted water to a boil. Add the
pasta, return to a boil, and
cook for 8–10 minutes, or until
tender but still firm to the bite.
Drain, refresh in a bowl of cold
water and drain again.

2 Place the radicchio and
oak leaf lettuce leaves
in a large bowl. Halve the
pears, remove the cores, and
dice the flesh. Toss the diced
pear with 1 tablespoon of
lemon juice in a small bowl to
prevent discoloration. Top the
salad with the Stilton, walnuts,
pears, pasta, tomatoes, onion
slices, and grated carrot. Add
the basil and corn salad.

3 Mix the remaining
lemon juice and the
olive oil and vinegar together
in a measuring cup, then
season to taste with salt and
pepper. Pour the dressing over
the salad, toss, and serve.

pasta salad with curry dressing

serves 4   **prep: 10 mins**   **cook: 10 mins**

You can make this salad well in advance and it would be a good accompaniment to serve at a barbecue party.

INGREDIENTS

4 oz/115 g dried farfalle

4–5 large lettuce leaves

1 green bell pepper, seeded and chopped

1 red bell pepper, seeded and chopped

2 tbsp chopped fresh chives

4 oz/115 g white mushrooms, chopped

DRESSING

2 tsp curry powder

1 tbsp superfine sugar

½ cup corn oil

¼ cup white wine vinegar

1 tbsp light cream

NUTRITIONAL INFORMATION

Calories 356

Protein 5g

Carbohydrate 28g

Sugars 7g

Fat 26g

Saturates 3g

---

variation

Replace the farfalle with other pasta shapes such as penne, fusilli, or conchiglie and use cremini mushrooms instead of the white ones, if you prefer.

cook's tip

If making this salad a few hours in advance, do not add the curry dressing to the salad until just before serving, otherwise it may go soggy.

1 Bring a large heavy-bottom pan of lightly salted water to a boil. Add the pasta, return to a boil, and cook for 8–10 minutes, or until tender but still firm to the bite. Drain, rinse in a bowl of cold water, and drain again.

2 Line a large bowl with the lettuce leaves and tip in the pasta. Add the green and red bell peppers, chives, and mushrooms.

3 To make the dressing, place the curry powder and sugar in a small bowl and gradually stir in the oil, vinegar, and cream. Whisk well and pour the dressing over the salad. Toss and serve.